PENGUIN BOOKS

ON BEING AWESOME

Nick Riggle dropped out of high school to become a pro skater, participating in stunt shows, demos, and world-class competitions (including three ESPN X Games). He has a BA in philosophy from UC Berkeley and a PhD from New York University, America's leading philosophy program; he is currently a philosophy professor at the University of San Diego. He speaks widely at conferences and workshops and co-organized the first major academic conference on the philosophy of street art and graffiti. He continues to publish in notable philosophy journals, as well as more popular outlets, including *McSweeney's*, *Aeon* (on the high five, awesomeness, and suckiness), and *Hyperallergic*. His current academic work focuses on the role of aesthetic value in human life and is supported by a grant from the Experience Project, a $4.8 million, three-year initiative at the University of North Carolina at Chapel Hill and the University of Notre Dame.

ON BEING

AWESOME

A Unified Theory of

How Not to Suck

NICK RIGGLE

PENGUIN BOOKS

PENGUIN BOOKS
An imprint of Penguin Random House LLC
375 Hudson Street
New York, New York 10014
penguin.com

Illustrations by Amanda Jaquin

LIBRARY OF CONGRESS CATALOGING-IN-PUBLICATION DATA
Names: Riggle, Nick, author.
Title: On being awesome : a unified theory of
how not to suck / Nick Riggle.
Description: New York : Penguin Books, 2017.
Identifiers: LCCN 2017016020 (print) | LCCN 2017024527
(ebook) | ISBN 9781524704681 (ebook) | ISBN 9780143130901
Subjects: LCSH: Success. | Conduct of life.
Classification: LCC BJ1611.2 (ebook) | LCC BJ1611.2 .R5175 2017
(print) | DDC 158.1—dc23
LC record available at https://lccn.loc.gov/2017016020

Printed in the United States of America
1   3   5   7   9   10   8   6   4   2

Set in Adobe Caslon Pro
Designed by Katy Riegel

to biz

Contents

A person only plays when they are a person in the full sense of the word, and they are fully a person only when they play.

—FRIEDRICH SCHILLER

There is no conflict between the individual and the social instincts, any more than there is between the heart and the lungs: the one the receptacle of a precious life essence, the other the repository of the element that keeps the essence pure and strong.

—EMMA GOLDMAN

If you obey all the rules, you miss all the fun.

—KATHARINE HEPBURN

SOCIA

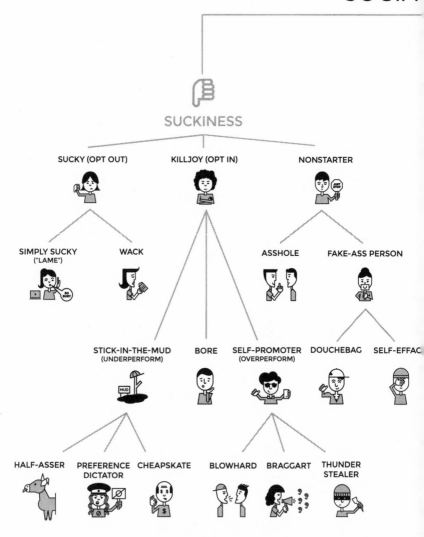

OPENING

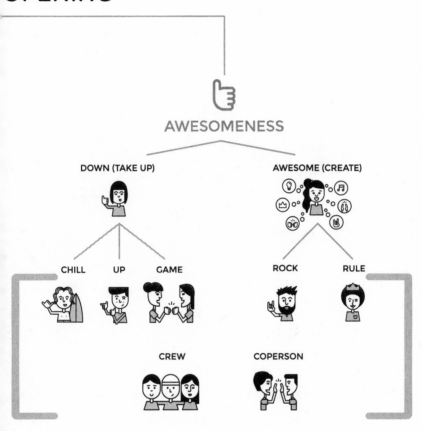

AWESOMENESS

DOWN (TAKE UP)

AWESOME (CREATE)

CHILL   UP   GAME

ROCK   RULE

CREW

COPERSON

SUCKINESS *and* AWESOMENESS: A Taxonomy

Chapter 1

In Search of Awesomeness

DURING HALFTIME AT a Boston Celtics basketball game in 2009, the Bon Jovi song "Livin' on a Prayer" came blasting through the loudspeakers. As people relaxed in their seats, chatting, eating, and drinking, the stadium's Fancam zeroed in on the audience, projecting their images onto the jumbo screen for everyone to see. Most of them did what fans normally do— they nudged their friends, smiled, waved, covered their faces, pointed to the giant images of themselves lording over the arena. But before long, the camera settled on Jeremy Fry, a skinny, ordinary young man, apparently there with his mother.

Fry could have reacted like everyone else. He could have smiled at the camera, nudged his mom and laughed, waved to friends who might be watching at home. Or he could have done nothing at all. But instead, he bounced out of his seat and

immediately assumed the role of Jon Bon Jovi in a music video—
lip-syncing, awkwardly dancing, and air-guitaring to the song
while roaming among and interacting with a diverse and increasingly lively crowd. Giant high fives, smooth 360s, fist pumps
to the beat, and arms in the air: his antics said, in loud effect,
Let's all pretend we're in a Bon Jovi music video! Soon the crowd
was joining in, cheering him on, and enacting various music
video roles.*

It is hard to describe the experience of watching Fry. It is en-
thralling, spirit lifting, inspiring. He's just *awesome*. That word is
used to describe him in YouTube comments dozens upon dozens
of times: "This is fucking awesome"; "This guy is awesome"; "This
guy is nothing but awesome"; "There are no words to describe how
awesome this guy is. Salut from Finland." Some comments even
suggest that Fry exhibits unadulterated awesomeness. We look
upon him with the kind of enthusiastic joy that might make us
bounce out of our seats and emulate him. Or more. At least one
commenter found a renewed faith in people: "This guy restored my
faith in humanity." Another saw in Fry the makings of a society-
structuring ideal: "This man should lead us."

And for many people in the crowd that is exactly what Fry
did. Much of his awesomeness seems to come down to the way
he proposed and orchestrated a performance that the crowd

---

* Are you near a smartphone or a computer? Watch the two-minute video by googling "HD
video of Jeremy Fry," or go to www.youtube.com/watch?v=mOHkRk00iI8. As I'm writing
this, the original video has 16.5 million views and counting.

enabled and then amplified, as women and men cheered him on, hugged him, gave him high fives, and lip-synced and air-guitared in unison. Many of them spontaneously, unreflectively, and enthusiastically accepted his proposal, breathing life into the collective effort. They might not have been as awesome as Fry, but they were consummately game.

However, as beautiful as the cooperative performance is, there's something puzzling about the overwhelmingly positive response and willingness to join in. Fry is a perfect stranger acting perfectly strangely. What exactly is so good or awesome about what he does? He is obviously not doing what one normally does in this context, and it's easy to imagine people who reasonably prefer to do just that. A few fans were predictably indifferent to or even slightly irked by Fry's animated proposal—they were there for the game, after all, and who is this weirdo, anyway? Although Fry had nearly the entire section of the stadium smiling, singing, and dancing along, there was one fan who roundly disapproved. Rather than ignore Fry, a man in a large blue T-shirt nudged him away. He even mimicked kicking him.

As many YouTube commenters observe, this guy totally sucks. Some go further and claim that he "represents everything that is wrong with the world." Others imagine speaking directly to him: "Dude get a life u suck."*

Even if you don't use the word *sucks* yourself, you probably

---

* He's also frequently called (perhaps incorrectly, as we will see in due time) a "douchebag" and an "asshole," among other far more inventive and colorful things.

hear it a lot. Suckiness, for better or worse, is on our minds, and like *awesome*, it's not a word reserved for the youthful set. In 2013, Wisconsin weather reporter Angelica Duria received cheers and a standing ovation from her on-air news team when, after six hours of reporting from a dreary snowscape, she summed up her findings: "It is snowing, and it *sucks here*." In 2014, Robert H. Lustig, professor of clinical pediatrics at the University of California, San Francisco, displayed full mastery of the term and even emphasized its special ability to articulate his thought:

> Now, I will tell you that America doesn't trust its politicians. And we have a good reason for that: they suck. If you don't quote me, I will be upset. The reason they suck is because, number one, they're interested in power, not doing the right thing, and, number two, they take money.*

Our political leaders are often called out as "sucky"—a fact that comedian George Carlin, as early as 2001, noted in his book *Napalm & Silly Putty*:

> Everybody says [politicians] suck. Well, where do people think these politicians come from? They don't fall out of the sky. They don't pass through a membrane from another reality. They come from American parents and American families, American

---

* German Lopez, "The Case for Treating Sugar like a Dangerous Drug," *Vox*, September 12, 2016, http://www.vox.com/2014/6/2/5771008/the-case-for-treating-sugar-like-a-drug.

homes, American schools, American churches, American businesses and American universities, and they are elected by American citizens. This is the best we can do folks. This is what we have to offer. It's what our system produces: Garbage in, garbage out. If you have selfish, ignorant citizens, you're going to get selfish, ignorant leaders. Term limits ain't going to do any good; you're just going to end up with a brand new bunch of selfish, ignorant Americans. So, maybe, maybe, maybe, it's not the politicians who suck. Maybe something else sucks around here . . . like, the public. Yeah, the public sucks. There's a nice campaign slogan for somebody: "The Public Sucks. Fuck Hope."*

Too much suckiness makes hope seem empty or absurd. Appeals to hope are more successful with politicians who openly acknowledge how much suckiness there really is; they appeal to our need to overcome it, to rise above and become awesome.

Just such hope was arguably part of then-senator Barack Obama's promise in 2008. Here he is in a joking (but not really) mood:

If I had to name my greatest strength, I guess it would be my humility. Greatest weakness, it's possible that I'm a little too awesome.†

* George Carlin, *Napalm & Silly Putty* (New York: Hachette, 2001).
† Senator Barack Obama, "Barack Obama at the Al Smith Dinner," Real Clear Politics, http://www.realclearpolitics.com/articles/2008/10/barack_obama_at_the_al_smith_d.html.

Obama seemed to appreciate the fact that the promise of awe-someness sang to the contemporary American spirit. It made his appeal to hope in 2008 seem irresistible to so many people. Could someone *that* awesome really be president? Saxophone-slinging Bill Clinton was cool; people wanted to have a beer with their bro George W. But fist-bumping Obama was just *awesome*. I was emphatically among the 69.5 million voters who thought, "This man should lead us."

•

The word *awesome* is, of course, the contemporary antonym of *sucks*. Some take this to be a condemnation of both terms, on the grounds that their usage is so broad that they're nearly empty or pointless, meaning little more than "good" and "bad" or, even worse, "I like that" and "I don't like that." As one jour-nalist recently noted, "The real problem with 'suck' is that it has become the antonym of 'awesome,' which has similarly replaced all adjectives of approval."* And a cursory look at how these terms are used might seem to confirm the point. Just consider the range of things that we casually call "awesome": a game, a social media app, a friend's behavior, the restaurant down the street, the concert last night, ourselves. And apparently nearly

---

* Frank Cerabino, "Cerabino: Bravo, ESPN: 'Sucks' Has Lost Its Succulence," *Palm Beach Post*, December 12, 2013, http://www.palmbeachpost.com/news/news/bravo-espn-sucks-has-lost-its-succulence/ncJth/.

anything can "suck," including, by Carlin's comedic lights, the whole of American society and culture.

It's easy to dismiss a glib "awesome" or facile "sucks" as trendy and ephemeral forms of speech. It is even easier to dismiss them if we regard their contemporary use as a lamentable and superficial co-opting of what should be powerful words. The philosophical comedian Louis C.K. comments:

[W]e waste the shit out of our words. It's sad. We use words like "awesome" and "wonderful" like they're candy. It was awesome? Really? It inspired *awe*? It was wonderful? Are you serious? It was full of *wonder*? You use the word "amazing" to describe a goddamn sandwich at Wendy's. What's going to happen on your wedding day, or when your first child is born? How will you describe it? You already wasted "amazing" on a fucking sandwich.

As tempting as it might be to share this attitude, even brief reflection on the meaning and use of *awesome* and *sucks* suggests that they capture something special: The threat of being a sucky person seems distinctive, and the promise of being awesome seems to resonate, at least with the US imagination, in a way that the thought of goodness, virtue, politeness, dutifulness, and other traditional forms of moral excellence do not. *Awesome* and *sucks* are powerful words on the contemporary tongue, and we have something important to learn—about ourselves, our culture, and our social aspirations—by resisting the impulse to spurn and dismiss them.

The contemporary resonance of *awesome* is evident across the vast landscape of American culture. We see it in our films and commercials, we hear it in our songs, and we feel it in our bones. "Everything is awesome," as Tegan and Sara sing in *The Lego Movie* (2014), which grossed nearly $500 million globally. "*Awesome* sells" might even be the new "Sex sells." An "awesome" sandwich is so much more enticing than one that is "very good" or "excellent," and this is reflected in the way *awesome* is used in commercial and popular culture.* It appears in all variety of marketing, from food and insurance commercials to all-purpose cleaners, wet wipes, and right wing political books—the subtitle of Ann Coulter's 2016 book, *In Trump We Trust*, is (ironically) "E Pluribus Awesome!" It seems that no matter what our political views are, we think our ethical unity as a nation is not *really* secured unless the public doesn't suck and hope isn't fucked—unless we are *awesome together.*

Of course, being awesome and not sucking does not rule out the more traditional forms of ethical excellence. It's not that we don't care about being fair and just, good and true; we don't want to be immoral, unprincipled, or vicious—quite the opposite: We want to love our neighbor; we are generally proud of whatever virtue we possess. And as we will see, awesomeness is

---

* See my Instagram account @onbeingawesome for a kind of "anthropology of awesome" that documents the use of *awesome* and *sucks* in commercial and popular culture.

threatened where justice and equality are not widespread and firm. The problem is that the thought of being virtuous or dutiful out of a love of virtue or duty doesn't readily stoke the twenty-first-century ethical imagination. But the thought of being awesome out of a love of awesomeness does. At the end of the day, what we ultimately want is to not suck. More than that: We want to be awesome.

•

But what exactly is being awesome? Why have these terms seized our hearts and minds? Do we really want to stoke fires of awe in the hearts of everyone we encounter, or be moved to awe by every band we hear and every sandwich we swallow? Why are we so fascinated by awesomeness, so irked by suckiness? Why do we care about being awesome and not sucking right now, in the early twenty-first century?

Although our fascination with awesomeness and suckiness is new, it is developed enough to be nuanced in ways that often go unappreciated. The terms *sucks* and *awesome* are conceptually related to a wide range of other terms we use. Notice that being "wack" is different from being a killjoy or an obnoxious self-promoter, but they all are ways of sucking. And being "down" is not quite the same as being "game" or "chill," but they both have something to do with awesomeness—at the very least they're both ways of being, for lack of a better term, non-sucky.

This brings us to a second compelling reason to seek a better understanding of awesomeness and suckiness. In addition to being distinctive, perhaps even new (or newly important) values, they bear conceptual connections to other ways of thinking and valuing that we care about—connections whose subtleties and nuances we don't quite understand. There is an enormous middle ground between being awesome and being flat-out sucky. What is the difference between being down and being game, and how do they relate to awesomeness? What exactly is sucky about being wack or being a self-promoter? Why are they *both* ways of sucking?

We can take the very first step toward answers to these questions by carefully considering the many ways we use the word *sucks*. Eventually we will do the same with *awesome*, but that will take more time to develop, in part because we have to carefully distinguish the contemporary significance of *awesome* from its traditional meaning of "awe-inspiring." The grammar of *sucks* is clear enough: It's a quippy and concise monosyllabic intransitive verb, far superior in pith and punch than a predicate adjective ("That is bad") or attributive adjective and noun ("That is a bad thing"). "That sucks!" gets right to the point.

Grammar aside, we use *sucks* in several different ways that need to be teased apart before we can make progress. My toaster sucks because it doesn't properly toast bread, which is the only thing it is really supposed to do. It sucks because it doesn't perform the way toasters are designed to perform. So some things suck because they fail to do what they are designed, supposed, or expected to do.

Sometimes *sucks* is used in a similar way to dismiss entire people or kinds of people, not merely a person's action. It's hardly worth naming names—we all have our favorite examples—but there are plenty of people to call out. These people, or at least their public personas, are hurricanes of ethical dysfunction and distortion; they're mean, unhinged materialists, aggressively confused, or soaringly arrogant and greedy. It seems that a person "sucks" in this sense if they fail to meet basic ethical standards, ones we expect every person to meet.

But we use *sucks* to apply to people in another way too, not only to evaluate, criticize, or wholly dismiss them. People can suck without being sucky people, just as a person can do something mean or nice without being a mean or nice person. Just because your friend bailed on you once, it doesn't mean he's a sucky *person*. He just kind of sucked that one time. He did a sucky thing. It's more illuminating to focus on how those who aren't sucky people can suck, because when we correctly use *sucks* to evaluate or dismiss a whole person rather than one of their actions, we can lose sight of precisely what makes them suck. It's often because of how they act, but it can be hard to zero in on it when so much of what they do sucks. It's easier when we look at the sucky actions of someone who is not a sucky person; their suckiness stands out in contrast to their general non-suckiness.

When an otherwise decent person does something sucky, it is not that they are sucking *at* one thing or another. Most people suck at something or other: bowling, dancing, drawing—I could go on. Yet we continue with our lives assuming that this doesn't mean that we suck *as a person* (or *at* being a person). There are basic standards or rules that you have to follow to do an activity well, and if you consistently cannot follow the rules or meet the standards, then you suck at it. It's probably not your fault, either. We can't be good at everything, and those who *are* can definitely suck. Most of us are stuck with sucking at one thing or another.

Suckiness is different.

And it is not a matter of sucking *at life*. People who suck at life don't necessarily suck, even if they are a little more likely to. Lots of artists, musicians, or comedians suck at life but are gloriously non-sucky people. Sucking at life is something we have all done at one point or another, by not really tackling the various things we have to do to have a life—regular laundry, paying bills on time, being a decent family member, watering the plants, basic personal hygiene. And sometimes our pursuits are too demanding, our luck too spare, or our culture too rigid, unaccommodating, or just plain shitty to allow us to be good at life *and* spend it doing things that don't suck.

Furthermore, people who don't suck at life can certainly suck. We all know people who have life basically figured out but who still suck nonetheless and perhaps all the more. They have good jobs, solid paychecks, mainstream prestige—and they walk into a room and suck the life right out of it. The American writer John Steinbeck notes that it's "strange how one person can saturate a room with vitality, with excitement. Then there are others . . . who can drain off energy and joy, can suck pleasure dry and get no sustenance from it. Such people spread a grayness in the air about them."* And they can do that in different ways. They might be tactless self-promoters, fake-ass people, sticks-in-the-mud, douchebags, thunder stealers, wet blankets, blowhards, or bores, among other things.

To better understand these different ways of sucking, we need to understand what it is for a person's action to suck. And once we do, then maybe we can understand what it is for someone to *not* suck, which will shed light on the special character of people who walk into a room (or stand up at halftime) and inject life into it. They're game, down, chill—they're just *awesome*. This will help us understand what it really means to be awesome, and how these different ways of sucking, not sucking, and being awesome fit together.

•

The task is urgent because when there's too much suckiness, it's hard not to feel Carlin's sense of hopelessness—which makes it hard not to suck hard. Often when we suck it's because we don't

---

* John Steinbeck, *Travels with Charley: In Search of America* (New York: Penguin Books, 1997), 37.

have the motivation *not* to suck, because it's sucked out of us by sucky people: a bore who can't appreciate your generosity and spirit; a lackluster friend who says she'll come to the party but doesn't; a miserable coworker who steals your thunder or can't talk about anything but himself. When you have to deal with these people, you may wonder why you should bother thinking up an awesome plan for your friends or your community. Why envision a road trip, cook a special meal, or throw a party? Why conjure a thoughtful surprise? Why rule? Why be down, game, or chill? Why be a breeze of sweet and pure awesomeness if some vacuum salesman is always knocking at your door?

As we explore the meaning, structure, history, and influence of awesomeness and suckiness, we will come to see that awesomeness matters a great deal, and there's good reason to do what we can to strive for, promote, and celebrate it. The aspiration to be awesome is, in a sense, an American phenomenon, but it can take hold almost anywhere. We will find awesomeness in a grieving guy in a Superman costume, in shovels made out of melted guns, in swings installed in bus stops, and in a range of emerging cultural practices, from social art to street skating. We will cast new light on our cultural history and our social future by looking at the cultural revolution of the 1960s, the invention of the high five, and the emergence of "cool" in the 1930s, among other things.

The idea I develop in this book is that our love of awesomeness is an expression of our hope for a better social culture—one that is more imaginative, creative, and communal, and one that promises to bolster, enhance, and even help to realize the kind of free, just, equal, and diverse society we aspire to. Our love of awesomeness emerged from our collective exploration and slow discovery of ways to bring community and connection back into a burgeoning individualistic culture, but without destroying that culture—indeed, while promoting and celebrating it.

After exploring the theory of what it is to be awesome and what it is to suck, we will be able to see how important these concepts are in our lives and how they inform some of our deepest social and even personal aspirations.

Maybe it's obvious, but I hope this book doesn't suck—I hope it's a step in the direction of greater awesomeness. Once we clearly understand what awesomeness and suckiness are and why they matter so much to us, we will be better at recognizing them in ourselves, in each other, and in our social and cultural ways of life. I hope a little intellectual, philosophical effort can bring us together around a common understanding, one that sheds light on being awesome and not sucking, and can maybe even make our world a little more awesome.

Chapter 2

A Theory

I F YOU WANT to understand something that seems too immense to comprehend—truth, beauty, knowledge, love, awesomeness, suckiness—it often helps to begin by trying to understand typical, simple, or uncontroversial examples. Try to formulate a theory about them, or state a few good principles, and then gradually bring in more complicated or marginal examples to see whether your theory or principles hold up.

For example, imagine that you are trying to understand the nature of beauty. It's usually a good idea to begin by thinking about clearly beautiful things, or things that people tend to agree are beautiful, like sunsets or classical sculpture. And when you have some good ideas about what makes these things beautiful, you can begin to consider more difficult cases, like abstract painting, minimalist music, or "social practice" art.

Jeremy Fry's grand gesture at the Celtics game is awesome, but it is also a fairly unique event. Focusing on it too much can make awesomeness seem rare and difficult. But it's not. There is the potential for awesomeness and suckiness in many of our simplest, everyday interactions—so let's start there.

Social Openings

Consider how you might normally order a coffee at your local café:

> **Employee:** Hi, what can I get for you today?
> **You:** I would like a large coffee, please.
> **Employee:** All right, that'll be two dollars, please.
> **You:** Here you go.
> **Employee:** Here *you* go. Have a nice day!
> **You:** Thanks. You too.

There is nothing remarkable about this interaction, which simply follows familiar conventions of consumer exchange. The employee plays his role as employee, and you play yours as coffee shop customer. It's not very different, aside from the happy influence of caffeine, from any other civil interaction. It's not very different from the kinds of actions that take place when we ask for directions, help someone carry something, or simply walk down the street. In each case, we act in our generic role as cashier, customer, helpful citizen, or person in public—we all tend to do what the social norms say we should do in these roles.

Our social norms largely determine the ways we act when we fall into certain standard roles, but in doing so, we tend to act in a generic manner. Your actions as a coffee shop customer are more or less the same as mine, provided we're both competent and know our manners. As the prolific and inventive writer and philosopher Iris Murdoch tells us, "We are not always the individual in pursuit of the individual. . . . Often, for instance when we pay our bills or perform other small everyday acts, we are just 'anybody' doing what is proper or making simple choices for ordinary public reasons."*

If someone asked you why you ordered coffee the way you did, you would give an ordinary public reason: "Well, that's just what one does to order a coffee. We don't stand on our heads or use a megaphone." We internalize vast amounts of information about what one "normally" does as a coffee shop customer, citizen in public, and so on, and we draw on this information to coordinate with each other or to simply get through the day more smoothly than we otherwise would.

But as a result, our actions don't reveal much about who we are as individuals. If we were wearing the same clothes and makeup, then nothing would distinguish us aside from our natural appearance, which, in and of itself, normally doesn't

---

* Iris Murdoch, *The Sovereignty of Good* (New York: Routledge, 2001), 41.

express a whole lot. Your individuality is constituted by your aspirations, your cherished beliefs, what you love and value, your sense of humor, your talents, whether you're shy or intense, your taste in food, music, and clothes, and so on. In other words, your individuality is what makes you *you* to yourself. It is composed of your appreciable features, which are those aspects of yourself that you cherish, want to cultivate, and want to explore, express, and share. But they are also the ones that it makes sense to value—the ones that really are worthy of appreciation, cultivation, and exploration.

Sometimes we abandon the ordinary public reasons and break out of the social roles. Sometimes we do so because we're forced to (in an emergency, for example) or because we're inattentive or impolite. Yet other times we break out of these roles by expressing our individuality. In doing so, we morph into Murdoch's "individual in pursuit of the individual."

When we break out of our norm-governed roles by expressing ourselves, we can create what I call a *social opening*. A social opening occurs when an opportunity arises to step outside of or creatively expand upon these roles—in particular, when there is a chance to recognize each other's individuality beyond whatever generic traits and skills are required to simply enact the social role or adhere to the social norms.

Social openings allow us to express ourselves, but social norms aren't the only things they allow us to transcend. They also function to break up our own everyday habits, prejudices, and routines—ones that aren't necessarily governed by social norms. We could call them our "personal norms." You might break a personal norm by talking to someone you wouldn't normally talk to, cooking a special meal for your family, going out of your way to help a stranger, sending a friend a gift just because, or spending the day learning to play the guitar or paint. Social openings give us an opportunity to step outside of our norms, social habits, and everyday routines by allowing us to explore and express our individuality with one another. Social openings are therefore also a kind of *self*-opening, because they can provide opportunities for self-expression, exploration, cultivation, and appreciation.

So how can we create social openings? Normally, someone deliberately creates one by expressing themselves. Consider a slight variation on the morning conversation with the coffee shop employee:

Employee: Hi, what can I get for you today?
You: I would like a large coffee, please.
Employee: All right, that'll be two dollars, please.
You: Small price to become human again. Here you go.
Employee: . . .

Here you have created a little social opening by breaking the norms, going off script, and making a little joke. In doing so, you give the employee an opportunity to recognize your sense of play and humor and react with a response of his own. You thereby give him a chance to break out of his role and express *his* individuality in response. If he takes up your offering in the right way, then the result is a kind of mutual appreciation of individuality. Offering the joke is a way of opening the door to this kind of appreciative interaction. Social openings are a success when this kind of appreciation occurs.

Social openings engage our capacity for self-expression and interpersonal appreciation, from the simple ability to smile at the right time or crack a joke to impressive gestures of creative generosity. There are many means of expression that allow us to break out of our social roles and norms: remarks (compliments, jokes), gestures (making faces, flashy movements), offerings (gifts), acts of kindness, playfulness, and displays (outfits), to name a few.

Imagine if you were to compliment the employee on his skills or clothes, make a silly face, do a little dance, offer a generous tip, or show up at the register with a sweet outfit—maybe you're going to a party, or feel experimental that day, or just feel like flaunting it. These would all give the employee an opportunity to acknowledge you for who you are in a way that reveals who he is. He might laugh at your joke or respond with his own, thereby revealing his sense of humor. He might notice your tip and make you a special drink or reciprocate by smiling at you (thereby revealing his perceptiveness and generosity). He might take up your invitation to notice what you're wearing and compliment your style.

Of course, not all such gestures are successful or appropriate. Attempts to create social openings can misfire in various ways, particularly when the individual you present is, in one way or another, off-putting. Suppose that instead of making a joke, you burp and smile. In doing so, you present yourself in a way that is distasteful (to most people, though I've known a few burp aficionados who might appreciate the offering). Your action is off-putting, and this gives the employee a reason not to engage. Now imagine you approach the employee and make an offensive joke. In this case, the way you present yourself to him gives him a reason to criticize you, which eliminates the possibility of mutual appreciative regard. Finally, suppose you are extremely friendly to the employee, as if you were good friends but you aren't. Here you show your friendliness, but in a way that suggests you may be presumptuous or deluded, or even needy. To him, this is evidence that you won't be accurately receptive to who he is, or that you are unaware of boundaries of personal comfort, and now he has reason not to engage. In short, success in creating social openings requires that you be sensitive to (1) the ways in which you break or set aside the social norms, and (2) the appeal of the individual you present, which in turn requires that you be aware of context and sensitive to the individual to whom you are expressing yourself.

Sometimes people deliberately break the social norms without creating a social opening because in breaking the social norms, they aim only to edify or admonish their audience in a certain way. For example, imagine you are in an elevator and someone is talking too loudly. In order to highlight the illicit behavior, you might mimic them and also talk loudly—not to be funny or shocking but to make it obvious that doing so is against a norm that people ought to observe. Here you break the norms with the aim of getting people back in line with them, and so do not create a social opening.

However, social openings can be created around education, critique, enlightenment, or illumination. The great etiquette writer Emily Post, whose works contain a good amount of awesome wisdom, often put her elbows on the table at formal dinner parties to make fun of the rule that one shouldn't do that. This is a blatant violation of a norm, but coming from Emily Post it says, "Free yourself from the tyranny of elbowless dinner tables!" and creates a social opening that addresses both those who might defend this rule and those who would like to abandon it. The example illustrates a crucial point that we will take up in more detail later: When there is real tyranny or social disorder, breaking the norms can create a social opening of an entirely different order. Generally, social openings occur when the norm breaking is in the spirit of individual cultivation, exploration, and expression, and this spirit is compatible with critique, reform, and edification.

It is important to emphasize the "cultivation and exploration"

aspect of social openings. The notion of self-expression is a little misleading. I don't want to suggest that we all have a deter-
minate or concrete self that, every now and then, we decide to
express and hope that others appreciate it. Rather, the kinds of
things we do when we express ourselves—play, create, explore,
take risks, imagine, and so on—allow us to deepen our self-
understanding and appreciation. This, in turn, allows us to cultivate and refine our sense of self or individuality.

When I talk of the "mutual appreciation of individuality,"
this can mean two things: a state of appreciation directed either
at one or more features of individuality—for example, one's perceptiveness, talent, or sense of style or humor—or at the simple
fact of our being individuals in pursuit of individuality. What I
mean by "the simple fact" is that sometimes, as in the Jeremy
Fry episode, the focus of a social opening's mutual appreciation
is our *pure individuality*—our basic capacity to break out of
whatever norms, stereotypes, roles, or rules saddle us and just
act or *exist* in that space. The individual purely as such is a playful, empathetic, and perceptive seeker and appreciator of other
individuals. Individuals gain definition as they cultivate *ways* of
exploring, playing, and seeking that they like and value—they
gain not just the ability to laugh, but a sense of humor; not just
the ability to empathize, but a refined sense of care and concern.

Now suppose you successfully create a social opening—you
don't alienate or offend anyone, and you aren't out to merely

admonish. What happens? The result of a successful social opening is a community, however small, of mutually appreciative individuals. English arguably lacks a term for the connections we form when this kind of mutual appreciation occurs—on the subway or bus, at concerts, barbecues, dinners, sporting events, and so on. We connect with people who aren't (yet anyway) really friends; they might become friends, or we might go our separate ways. Calling them our fellows, companions, or buddies doesn't necessarily capture the kind of mutual feeling that can develop in such situations. In some cases, a lovelike emotion can emerge, leaving us with a sense of connection and joy—one that can be a pathway to a deeper love and lasting connection, one that is meaningful even when fleeting. We never leave a social opening unchanged. We leave with stories and insights, challenged stereotypes and strengthened bonds, deepened empathy and opened minds.

Let's say that a *co-person* (or *coperson*) is someone with whom you have formed a mutual appreciative regard directed at the individual each is. When social openings are created and carried off, copersons are created on the small and large scale—from the mutual appreciation between you and a coffee shop employee to the complex web of mutual appreciation at a social event, concert, or spontaneous gathering. Let's call a group of copersons—paradigmatically, a group of regular copersons—a *crew* (or *squad*).

The Basics of Suckiness

So how would you react if you were to present someone with a social opening and they refused to accept it? Imagine that the employee from the previous interaction recognizes that you created a social opening, but for no apparent reason deflects or dismisses it:

> **Employee:** Hi, what can I get for you today?
> **You:** I would like a large coffee, please.
> **Employee:** All right, that'll be two dollars, please.
> **You:** Small price to become human again. Here you go.
> **Employee:** Um. Here's your coffee.

That sucks! He could accept your social opening, but he refuses. By saying "Um," he recognizes that you're acting out of the defined role of coffee customer and closes the social opening thereby offered. To be fair, coffee shop employees would have to be social virtuosos to engage with every caffeine-addled brain who wants to chat or issue a silly joke. What matters here is the *inclination* to think that the café employee sucks when he rejects your social opening, even if you should resist the inclination in similar cases. When someone is busy, overworked, or clearly exhausted, a better way to create a social opening, if at all, might be to just tell them how awesome they are. An acquaintance was at the airport observing an airline employee doing an incredible job handling luggage and responding to a flood of irritated passengers. He went out of his way to compliment the worker on a job well done. Their response was a solid high five (awesome) and a return to work.

Sucking is, first and foremost, a matter of *being able but refusing to take up social openings.* Social openings are essentially opportunities for the mutual appreciation of individuality, allowing us to express, attribute, and cultivate our individuality beyond whatever is required to play out the script written in the social code, or to carry on in our everyday habits and routines. People who suck in this sense refuse to play along even though they could.

Your joke gave the café employee an opportunity to acknowledge your sense of humor. He could have acknowledged you by saying something as simple as "You're funny," or he could have reciprocated by playing off of your joke and saying something weird or quirky, like "WE ARE ALL ROBOTS HERE" in a robot voice. But he made it clear that he didn't care.

At the very least, the employee could have been merely polite. He could have mustered a polite laugh or offered a well-wishing smile. Politeness in this context is neither sucky nor non-sucky—it's a way of opting out of awesomeness without really sucking. The merely polite person does not act from a sense of their own individuality; rather, they act out of a sense of their *common humanity*, their sense of respect for all people, and this is a sense of self we can all tap into. We might say that the merely polite person "entertains" the social opening without taking it up in all its glory. However, as we will see in chapter 4, people who are *always* merely polite are in danger of sucking.

Let's be more specific about what makes an action suck. Sucky actions are a response to a certain kind of opportunity—an opportunity to present, acknowledge, and cultivate each other's individuality on the small and large scales. This is the heart of suckiness—and, logically speaking, part of the structure of awesomeness—so we need to be as clear and specific as we can. For your action to suck, it must meet the following conditions.

1. You encounter a social opening.

The first condition for an action to suck says that you must encounter a social opening. It doesn't state that someone must present you with a social opening. Social openings can occur without either of the people for whom they occur intentionally creating them.

Imagine you're walking down the street, and just as you're passing someone walking the other way a remarkable event occurs—a pigeon flies just inches from your face, or a gust of wind nearly knocks you over. These are remarkable events, ones that each of you knows the other recognizes, and recognizes as worthy of comment. If neither of you says something—if you just walk by without acknowledging each other, making a joke, or smiling—then you've missed an opportunity and you suck a little.

2. *You recognize the opportunity.*

People who suck recognize the opportunity for a social opening but don't act on it. They see that their social conditions are unusual relative to the social norms—that someone has broken out of or creatively riffed on a social norm in a way that invites a positive response. But it is possible to fail to *recognize* that such a thing has happened. If that's true then you don't suck. You might *seem* to suck, but you don't. You don't because, for whatever reason, you just failed in that instance to see what was going on. Sometimes we are simply aloof, stressed out, or too preoccupied with important business to recognize when we have encountered a social opening.

That said, there are certain standards of perceptiveness that we demand of most people. Other things being equal, you should notice your friend's new haircut; you should be aware of someone's clear attempt at humor. You can suck when you are insensitive to social openings because you are *gratuitously* aloof or *unreasonably* stressed. More generally, we should be aware of individuals' expressive efforts. If you don't recognize a social opening because you failed to meet these standards (in spite of being able to meet them), then you suck.

3. *You* could *accept the opportunity* . . .

Even if you are faced with and recognize a social opening, you might not be able to take it up. Sucky people are in a position to take up the social opening but refuse. The thought here is that you suck only when you *could* take up the social opening, when there's really nothing stopping you from accepting the opportunity to express and appreciate, no really good reason to opt out.

Consider the coffee shop employee who seemed to suck. It is easy to imagine him being way too busy to do much more than focus on doing his job, on playing his practical role as a coffee shop employee. If he really were that busy, then he would be reasonably unable to accept the opportunity and he does not really suck. If that's his reason for not accepting, then it's a good one—it makes sense for him to opt out of the social opening he's offered (though he could have been more tactful and avoided the "um").

In contrast, suppose he closed your social opening for a different reason. Suppose he just didn't like the color of your shirt, felt like taking his bad day out on you, or superficially judged that you are too boring to be in his vicinity. In that case he sucks.

Another way to summarize the third condition is to say that we avoid suckiness only when we act on a good reason to opt out. Sucking is a matter of opting out of social openings for bad reasons.

But what if you decline a social opening for a bad reason

while *also* possessing a *good* reason for declining—maybe one that didn't occur to you at the time? For example, consider what we should say about a coffee shop employee who really is extremely busy, and so has a good reason to opt out of a social opening—but who does so because he doesn't like the color of your shirt. There's a sense in which, by his lights in that moment, he could have accepted the social opening—he knows that individuals are so much more than the color of their shirt, so that is not a good enough reason to opt out. But in fact, in the broader scheme of things, his extreme busyness gave him a good enough reason. In this case I think we should say that the person is being unnecessarily sucky. He has lost sight of his legitimate reason for opting out and fallen into a pit of suckiness.

4. . . . *but you don't.*

This is the heart of sucky action: It's a matter of being able to accept social openings you encounter and recognize but simply blowing them off for no good reason.

But why should we take up the social openings we encounter? You may be thinking, "I might have no good reason to opt out of a social opening, but why does that mean I have to accept it or else be labeled 'sucky'? If my reason to refuse is no good, then why does that mean I ought to accept?"

There are two basic reasons that favor opting in to social openings. They are usually in play for us when we are being awesome and not sucking, but when your reasons for opting out are bad or weak, those reasons take center stage.

The first has to do with our desire to cultivate, express, and explore our individuality. We want to express ourselves, test and develop our interests, engage our tastes, sensibilities, and style. Social openings are paradigmatic opportunities to engage this interest by engaging our pure or developed individuality (in some cases only in a small, fleeting, but nonetheless valuable way). And this is something that we cannot do alone—we need others to help us along, take up our offerings, and show us how to be awesome and not suck. This means that we also have an interest in promoting the individual engagement of others. By opting out for no good reason, you act as if you don't have these interests or as if being awesome doesn't really matter. But you do! And it does.

We could perhaps imagine a person who wholly lacks these interests. They don't care about being an individual and have no interest in promoting the individuality of others. They might be very risk averse, fully committed to being merely polite, or, more extremely, they might eschew all attempts at social humor, play, creativity, and so on. It's not that such a person couldn't exist, but they would be missing out on an enormous part of life. In a sense, they would be missing out on life itself, insofar as life isn't just a matter of having a heartbeat. Being invested in the pursuit of individuality is part of what it is to really live.*

---

* As the moral and political philosopher John Stuart Mill put it in *On Liberty* (New York: Penguin Classics), 2006, 68: "Human nature is not a machine to be built after a model, and

The second reason to opt in to social openings is that if your potential coperson succeeds in creating one, then they have thereby given you a reason to do so. In addition to the general interest in engaging your individuality, their joke merits laughter, their style impresses, their generosity moves, their creativity inspires, their invitation is intriguing, and so on.

As we will see in detail in chapter 4, suckiness is more complicated than this; there are many ways to suck, but these are the basics. By opting out of a social opening for no good reason you let yourself and your potential coperson down by failing to respond to these reasons of awesomeness. Of course, this doesn't mean that you are morally obligated to accept. It's not obvious that you're open to moral censure if you opt out for no good reason. You just kind of suck. The spirit of awesomeness does not flow within you, at least at that moment.

•

Some readers might cringe at the term *sucks*, thinking it refers to Rather Adult Things. And indeed some etymological claims about the term locate its origin in such things. In addition to the

set to do exactly the work prescribed for it, but a tree, which requires to grow and develop itself on all sides, according to the tendency of the inward forces which make it a living thing. . . . Such are the differences among human beings in their sources of pleasure, their susceptibilities of pain, and the operation on them of different physical and moral agencies, that unless there is a corresponding diversity in their modes of life, they neither obtain their fair share of happiness, nor grow up to the mental, moral, and aesthetic stature of which their nature is capable." Chapter III, "On Individuality, As One of the Elements of Wellbeing."

fellatio speculation, there is the thought that it derives from the expression "suck an egg," or perhaps from the expression "sucks hind teat" (which, come to think of it, we should probably revive).

But like so much etymology, these accounts are highly speculative, complicated, and unclear. And in a way, it doesn't matter. We can set the etymological speculation aside and focus on the special metaphor that our theory makes salient. Sucky people *suck the life out of things*. We create social openings with a certain hope or aspiration—one that we know speaks to something we all care about. We hope to foster the feeling of life and connection embodied in our copersons and crews. And when people refuse a social opening, they dash this hope. Sucky people prevent these feelings and bonds from emerging and developing and sometimes even replace them with their opposites, which range from frustration, ennui, and loneliness to alienation and despair.

The Basics of Non-Suckiness

Now that we understand the basics of suckiness, we can use our theory to illuminate what it is to not suck. Consider a person who:

1. is presented with a social opening;
2. recognizes the opportunity;
3. is able to accept the social opening; and
4. *accepts* it.

Far from sucking, this person is *down* or perhaps even *game*—
that is, *enthusiastically* down. She commits and opens herself up
to the interaction, breathing life into and completing the social
opening. On the most basic level, then, not sucking involves
regularly accepting social openings; the basics of not sucking
are a matter of being down.

As we will see later, just as there are many ways to suck,
there are a variety of ways to take up social openings and not
suck. Consider a variation on our coffee shop scenario:

Employee: Hi, what can I get for you today?
You: I would like a large coffee, please.
Employee: All right, that'll be two dollars, please.
You: Small price to become human again. Here you go.
Employee: Welcome back.

Here the employee takes up your social opening by playing
along, adopting your pretense and welcoming you back into the
human realm. Instead of being merely polite or dismissing your
social opening, he opts in and engages. This completes the social opening and secures the formation of copeople.

Articulating Awesome

So far our theory captures what it is to suck—it's to fail to take
up social openings. It also captures what it is to not suck—it's

to take up social openings. Now, what about people who excel at *creating* the social openings?

This is the heart of awesomeness.

Awesome people inject life into things: They create and carry out social openings, instituting communities and cultures in which people can develop, display, and appreciate the individual each other is or aspires to be.

Consider what happened when you walked into the coffee shop and decided not to simply enact the role of coffee shop customer. When you ordered coffee, you harnessed a motive that broke you out of the normal way of doing things; you expressed yourself in a way that created a social opening; your coperson was down, establishing the requisite mutual appreciation; and all was awesome.

We perform an awesome action when:

1. we approach a situation normally governed by a social role or norm;
2. the spirit of awesomeness flows within us;
3. we harness this motive and break out of (or creatively riff on) the social role or norm; and
4. we thereby create a social opening and give our copeople an opportunity to suck or not suck.

That's the basic, everyday case. Opportunities to be awesome in that way are ample. But awesome action can take this basic structure to another level—from inspired halftime she-nanigans to giant shifts in social structure. Awesome people are excellent at creating successful social openings. They are, therefore, skillful coperson creators: They are skilled at the awe-some art of crew building, of inspiring community and mutual positive regard. They are the overlords of interpersonal appreci-ation. They aren't always moral saints or masters of virtue, but they are the lifeblood of the coperson community.

In what follows we will refer to actions and people as being *awesome* when they are excellent at creating social openings. We will use *awesomeness* to refer to the state of affairs that ex-ists when a social opening is created, people are down, and co-persons are made, meaning the social opening is fully realized and successful. Awesomeness normally inheres in groups of individuals; it's a feature of collections of people in which some-one is being awesome and others take up the awesome person's social opening. In this way we might say, speaking a little loosely, that someone who is down is awesome because they made an essential contribution to awesomeness, even though they didn't exactly create the social opening.

Corniest insight in this book: The word *awesome* can be parsed as *a we* that is *so me*.

This illuminates why we think the Jeremy Fry performance is so awesome. His decision to wholeheartedly embody Bon Jovi and rock out broke with the conventions of halftime hang-ing. By breaking out of the role of basketball fan at the arena, he created a social opening that brought the entire section of the stadium together. The people who joined him were down or game—they took up the social opening that Fry created and did their part to institute awesomeness. And the infamous bro in blue sucks—he brazenly refused to take up the social opening. In fact, he disparaged and rejected it (more on that later).

Mixing It Up

As the Fry episode illustrates, suckiness and awesomeness can interact in a complex social opening. But sometimes a single person's action contains elements of both suckiness and awesomeness. And when that happens we're often unsure whether they have really created a social opening. Consider the actions of my kind and eccentric unicycle-riding junior high school science teacher, who was sort of awesome but in a slightly sucky way. Some mornings before classes began, he would ride a unicycle around the halls in a vaguely inviting but somewhat alienating way. In doing so, he created a social opening by breaking the normal course of the mornings at school, displaying his talents and introducing budding teens—who were more familiar with skateboards and inline skates—to such a foreign object. But although his method was well intentioned, it was out of touch. The vast majority of junior high school kids couldn't care less about unicycles—objects whose nerdy skittishness all too easily reminds preteens of their own awkwardness. And he wasn't tapping into a rich tradition whose value is important for twelve-year-olds to understand. The result was that he came off as alienating and unaware, if not a little self-absorbed. It was sort of awesome, but in a sucky way. (He was also fond of telling us in class, in a patronizing, science teacher tone, "People don't suck; only vacuums suck," which showed how little he understood suckiness.)

The lesson here is a general one, which we will dwell on at various points in the book: Success in creating social openings requires sensitivity to individuality. To repeat an earlier point, not all ways of breaking or creatively expanding on social roles and conventions create social openings. To intentionally create a social opening, you must express individuality that is worthy of appreciation. In some cases, as with my unicycle-riding teacher, it can be unclear whether the individuality expressed is worthy of appreciation; it can be a matter of uncertainty, disagreement, and debate. Some modes of individuality, such as a cultivated cynicism, scrappiness, or cheery optimism, appeal only to certain individuals. But in other cases it is clear.

Consider two racists who think they are creating a social opening with a clearly racist joke. One tells the joke; the other issues a high five while laughing. Isn't this awesomeness for racists? No, it's not. There is no such thing as Ku Klux Klan awesomeness because baseless hatred and bigotry are not features of individuality that are worthy of appreciation—quite the opposite, because awesomeness is rich and inclusive. Racists cannot form copeople under the banner of their bigotry. They might think they are doing so, and in some ways it might seem like they are, but they aren't. The same is true of other attempts to create community through exclusion; for example, bullies who team up to taunt someone they regard as inferior.

Understanding awesomeness helps us to further appreciate how sucking *at* something is different from sucking *as a person*. You might do something awesome while sucking at the very activity that makes you awesome. Imagine you're having a friend over and you know she loves a certain obscure dish that you have no idea how to make. But you try anyway. You go out of your way to find a good recipe, buy all the ingredients, and prep the kitchen and home for a warm and special meal. You spend hours chopping, sweating, putting it all together, only to emerge with something barely resembling food. You suck at making that dish. But you made it, or at least something resembling it, and that is awesome. So one can suck *at* something but nonetheless be awesome, which shows how little sucking at one thing or another has to do with awesomeness.

Why *Awesome*?

The word *awesome* as it resonates with us these days has new social meaning; it's used to talk about social openings and their dynamics. But why did we adopt this word to talk about such things? The traditional meaning of *awesome* is simply "awe-inspiring," or, to summarize most dictionary definitions, "inspiring a feeling of reverence or respect, often combined with wonder, fear, or apprehension." Something seems awesome in the traditional sense when it makes us feel that we are so small, the universe is so vast, and it's all just so wonderful, amazing, or overwhelming: a deep, dark, beautiful starry sky; a vast, open ocean; a great work of art; a stunning scientific theory.

But merely breaking a social norm or convention does not inspire a feeling of reverential wonder in us. Maybe it would in a country or culture where falling out of line carries a serious threat of violence. But in general we are not such die-hard rule followers that we stand in awe of people who break with or creatively expand upon a common convention or norm. And, though it sometimes might, breaking norms in a way that inspires community hardly merits the feeling that we are so awfully small and the universe so wonderfully vast.

Of course, *awesome* also has a widely recognized informal meaning, which American-English dictionaries commonly claim is just "excellent" or "extremely good." Although people certainly do use the word this way, the definition fails to capture the important difference between being excellent and being awesome, in the distinctive, contemporary sense of that word.

Many things can be excellent without being awesome: sports teams, bands, restaurants, TV shows—the list goes on. Consider a really good band, for example—one that is pitch-perfect, culturally astute, innovative, and enjoyable. Such a band can be excellent without being awesome. During a live show, they might simply display their excellence in a way that is to be enjoyed and appreciated, but without fostering mutual appreciative regard. Compare, for example, the live performances of the American rock band Grizzly Bear (excellent) and the late American folk singer and activist Pete Seeger (awesome). Grizzly Bear prefer not to "perform" for their audience and stick to a fairly minimal act in which they execute their intricate songs as perfectly as possible. Seeger, in stark contrast, sometimes barely even sang his songs, encouraging the audience to join in the performance. The result was often a room full of strangers singing together, with Seeger leading in enthusiastic strums, awesomely. Seeger had great faith in the awesomeness of music: "If there's a world here in a hundred years, one of the main reasons will be music. It can leap over barriers of politics and leap over barriers of religion and race. And people who never thought they'd be doing the same thing together will be listening and joining in on the same song."*

Awesomeness is a distinctive phenomenon, wherein someone expresses themselves in the spirit of fostering a coperson community—from creating a social opening at the local café to enlivening or enriching the community or workplace, throwing a great party, or getting a whole section of a stadium to play around.

---

* From the documentary *Greenwich Village: Music That Defined a Generation.* You can learn more about Seeger from the excellent 2007 documentary *Pete Seeger: The Power of Song.*

So why have we adopted the word *awesome* in these con-
texts? What possible connection could there be between *awe*
and *awesomeness*? Our feelings of awe often come along with
a certain desire to connect, share, or reach out. When we are
moved to awe by an album, a symphony, a novel, or a painting,
we want to tell our friends about it, post about it on social media, or give it as a gift. When we feel so small and wonderfully
overwhelmed, we want to band together under a common ae-
gis, which might be nothing more than feeling wonder, fear, or
apprehension *together.* By reaching out in these ways, we create
a social opening; we give our friends an opportunity to see and
feel what we are seeing and feeling. This suggests that awe tends
to inspire in us the desire to create social openings. Awe inspires us to be awesome.

Some empirical studies seem to confirm a strong connection
between feeling awe and the impulse to reach out, to share and
communicate that feeling. Researchers at the University of
Pennsylvania studied nearly seven thousand *New York Times*
articles to examine which ones were shared the most and why.*
They found that articles that evoke high emotional arousal (awe
or anger) are more "viral" than those with low emotional
arousal (sadness, for example). And among the positive emotions, the emotion of awe stood out as very strongly correlated
with sharing. Dr. Jonah Berger, one of the researchers, explains:

---

* Jonah Berger and Katherine L. Milkman, "What Makes Online Content Viral?" *Journal
of Marketing Research* 49, no. 2 (2012): 192–205.

"If I've just read this story that changes the way I understand the world and myself, I want to talk to others about what it means. I want to proselytize and share the feeling of awe. If you read the article and feel the same emotion, it will bring us closer together."*

If that's right, then it's no wonder we adopted *awesome* to talk about social openings. Our cultural interest in the value of creative social openings motivated a shift in our use of the word, from using it to talk about awe-inspiring things to using it to talk about the things that awe inspires—reaching out, connecting, sharing, and being closer together.

---

* John Tierney, "Will You Be E-mailing This Column? It's Awesome," *New York Times*, February 8, 2010, http://www.nytimes.com/2010/02/09/science/09tier.html?_r=0.

Chapter 3

The Ethics of Awesomeness

B EING AWESOME IS a matter of creatively breaking out of, or riffing on, norms that determine much of everyday life, and doing so in an expressive way, generating a social opening that allows for the mutual appreciation of individuality. This can happen in everyday life, on the bus or at your local coffee shop, and in more extraordinary situations. Awesome people excel at creating and sustaining social openings. They are *creative community builders*, whose inspired social insight and communal spirit promote coperson creation.

Creative community builders form the center of what I call the *ethics of awesomeness*, which concerns the actions, habits, character traits, values, and principles—in short, the ways of life—that make us awesome and not sucky. Their actions vividly demonstrate the subtlety, breadth, scale, ingenuity, and art of social opening creation. The ethics of awesomeness concerns (1) ways of being or learning from such a person; (2) ways of responding to such people or taking up, sustaining, and amplifying their social openings; (3) ways of failing to respond to or sustain social openings; and (4) forms of life, culture, and society that embody the ethos of awesome more generally.

In this chapter and the next we will develop the ethics of awesomeness, first in this chapter by focusing on aspect 1 and sketching its contours. Following that, in chapter 4, we will dig deeper and address aspects 2 and 3, looking in detail at the many ways of responding and failing to respond to social openings—from being down and game to being a killjoy, blowhard, fake-ass person, or just wack. This gives us a guide for navigating the ethics of awesomeness and suggests strategies for being more awesome and less sucky. Chapters 5 and 6 will address aspect 4 by looking first at the origins of awesome in American culture and then at emerging forms of culture that embody the spirit of awesomeness.

•

So what exactly is ethics? What is an ethical theory? Ethics is the philosophical study of good and bad actions; ethical theories are accounts of what makes actions good or bad. Most generally, ethics concerns how we should live—how we should or shouldn't act and how we should or shouldn't treat other people. This includes clearly moral questions about whether we should eat meat or support the death penalty, but it also covers questions about whether to have a beer with lunch, listen to music more often, or learn how to cook. In fact, the word *ethics* has roots in the Ancient Greek *ethos*, which means "character" and is used to describe the ways of life that define a community.

One of the most influential ethical theories, developed initially by the great Enlightenment philosopher Immanuel Kant (1724–1804), says (among other things) that you should always treat people, including yourself, with the utmost respect, and never merely as a tool to get something you want.* If you treat someone merely as a tool, according to Kant, then you fail to treat them as a reasoning, self-directed person, and that is ethically wrong. This is an ethical theory, or a proposal about what makes actions good or bad. Roughly, an action is good only when it is respectful and bad when it is disrespectful. For example, failing to pay someone for their work is bad because it fails to respect them and treats them as a mere tool.

Kant's ethics focuses on our obligations—what we ought to do—given the mere fact that we can ask, "What should I do?" The fact that we can ask this question implies that we can stand back from and consider our impulses and inclinations—we aren't always animated by pure instinct but by motives that are refined by

---

* "Act so that you use humanity, as much in your own person as in the person of every other, always at the same time as end and never merely as means." See his *Groundwork for a Metaphysics of Morals*, ed., trans. Allen W. Wood (New Haven, CT: Yale University Press, 2002).

thought and reflection. We can ask, "Would it suck if I never said hello to my neighbors?" or "That person over there is doing an impressive job. Would it be awesome to tell them that?" Kant thought that having this capacity to reflect on our actions is central to being a person, and when we do reflect well and act, we act excellently as persons rather than as purely instinct-driven animals. His ethics is largely about humans in pursuit of their humanity—humans in pursuit of their ability to respect and be respected—or, in other words, people in pursuit of their personhood.

But, as we have seen, awesomeness is about individuals in pursuit of individuality. The "ethics" of awesomeness, then, is a theory of how to act excellently not merely as a person who can reflect and respect but also as an individual in pursuit of individuality.

So what do you have to add to a person in pursuit of personhood to get an individual in pursuit of individuality? We cannot answer this question without calling on another philosophical subject: aesthetics, or the philosophy of art and beauty. It would be misleading to say that the theory we are developing is simply an ethical theory. The ethics of awesomeness is also, in a sense we will develop as we proceed, an *aesthetics* of awesomeness. Central to the ethics of awesomeness is a range of aesthetic categories, or categories that are essential to art or beauty: creativity, individuality, style, imagination, and play. Since these concepts are essential to understanding the ethics of individuals in pursuit of individuality, the theory we are developing is a kind of "aesthetic ethics," or an ethical theory that essentially and centrally involves the aesthetic.

In fact, things are even more complicated than this because of the way the ethics and aesthetics of awesomeness concern social life and community building. The ethics and aesthetics of being awesome are pitched in a sociopolitical register. For simplicity we will continue to speak of the "ethics of awesomeness," using *ethics* in its broadest ancient Greek–inspired sense, but we should keep in mind that awesomeness cannot be captured by ethics, aesthetics, or politics alone. It is best to think of awesomeness as its own category—one that has ethical, aesthetic, and social character.

The ethics of awesomeness is a view about how we can cultivate our individuality while building communities of mutually appreciative individuals. Thus, it is ultimately a view about how we can live well together. Ideally, a good ethical theory will inspire us to live by its lights; it will move us to see ourselves in a new way and compare how we live to how we might live if we were guided by the theory more often. So in that spirit we will look at various sources of inspiration that we might learn from and apply in our own lives and communities.

As we will see, the special character of the ethics of awesomeness derives from its social, creative, and communal focus. To begin, it will help to go back in time to 1977, to the origins of an action we strongly associate with awesomeness, the original grand gesture of being game: the *high five*.

The High Five

The pinnacle of Jeremy Fry's performance could very well be one of the most epic high fives ever spontaneously achieved. At 1:02 in the video you'll see a double fist pump followed by a resounding high five, which rapidly transforms into a tucked 360-degree spin, landed with arms open wide (to appreciate all of its glory, watch it in slow motion).

The perfectly executed classic high five is expressively superior to the traditional handshake. It involves more coordination and allows for variation and elaboration, and true success resounds with a loud *whoopash!* that communicates to others that a connection has been made and doubly affirmed.

The person widely credited with inventing the high five is Glenn Burke (1952–1995), a black baseball player and gay trailblazer, recognized by the Baseball Hall of Fame as Major League Baseball's first gay player.* On October 2, 1977, at Dodger Stadium, Dusty Baker had just hit his thirtieth home run of the season. Burke was up to bat next, and when Baker rounded third base and approached home plate, Burke was waiting to greet him. "His hand was up in the air, and he was arching way back," Baker recalls. "So I reached up and hit his hand. It seemed like the thing to do." Burke immediately went up to bat and proceeded to hit his first Major League home

---

* Radiolab's podcast *Patient Zero* discusses the complexities of the high five's origins.

run. When he made his way around the bases and rounded home plate, Baker was standing there with his hand up high.

Burke was an exemplar of awesomeness. According to sports agent Abdul-Jalil al-Hakim, "He was a joyous, gregarious person. He could high five you without necessarily going through the motion with his hand."* By all accounts, Burke was essential to the distinctive life and spirit of the mid-1970s Dodgers baseball club. When he was traded to the abysmal Oakland Athletics in 1978, the spirit of the team changed dramatically. Writer Jon Mooallem reports, "LA sportswriters described the trade as *sucking the life* out of the Dodgers' clubhouse. A couple of players were seen crying at their lockers."†

Many people think the high five signals the recognition of success or excellence, but as the story of Burke and Baker suggests, this rests on a slight confusion. Consider the confusion-generating fact that NBA players routinely high-five the guy who *misses* his free throws.‡ The players cannot be praising the free-thrower for his achievements or excellence. Rather, they are using it as Burke intended, to build and confirm community. Memphis Grizzlies forward Jon Leuer explains, "If you miss [a free throw], you want your teammates to say, 'Hey,

---

* Jon Mooallem, "The History (and Mystery) of the High Five," in *The Best American Sports Writing 2012*, ed. Michael Wilbon and Glenn Stout (Boston: Houghton Mifflin Harcourt Publishing, 2012).

† *Ibid.*; emphasis added.

‡ *The New York Times* reports on this and nicely captures the confusion: Scott Cacciola, "He Missed a Shot? Give That Man a Hand," *New York Times*, April 11, 2015, http://www.nytimes.com/2015/04/12/sports/basketball/he-missed-a-shot-give-that-man-a-hand.html.

I'm here for you.'"* What the high five expresses, at least in its original form, is not the mutual appreciation of achievement but the feeling we get upon the achievement of mutual appreciation.

Glenn Burke thought he experienced that feeling for the first time: "You think about the feeling you get when you give someone the high five. I had that feeling before everybody else."† Burke's thought is that the high five creates a new feeling of awesomeness. Whether or not a new feeling emerged along with the high five, and regardless of whether Burke felt it for the first time, we know what he's talking about: It's an affect-laden recognition of copersonhood, of success in creating or cultivating interpersonal connection—in short, of awesomeness.

The high five is a brilliant symbol of the ethics of awesomeness. The ideally awesome person is, like Burke, a virtuoso of communal imagination, imagining culture and community where it might not exist and using inventive action to bring it to life.

Creative Community Builders

Burke's and Fry's actions show that the ideally awesome person is a creative community builder. Burke not only brought his joy and love to a team, he made the team what it was and defined its very character as more than just a collection of baseball

---

* Ibid.
† Mooallem, "The History (and Mystery) of the High Five."

players—as a crew. And he did this in part by inventing the means by which they recognized and appreciated each other, the high five. Jeremy Fry's timing, creative insight, and expressive zeal established an almost irresistible social opening—one so powerful that it moved perfect strangers to play along. Glenn Burke used his charisma, exuberance, and high five; Jeremy Fry used his bold dance moves. Creative community builders use their ingenuity, insight, and courage to foster mutual appreciative regard.

The creative community builder doesn't create just any community—she creates a community of a special kind. This can get confusing because we use the word *community* in several different ways. At the very least, a community is a group of people who have a connection or similarity. But this minimal sense of community is too simple. All English speakers form a community by virtue of their shared language, but the Revolutionary War was between English speakers. And US citizens form a community by virtue of their shared citizenship, but the Civil War was a time of the utmost division. Even people who depend on one another, cohabitate, and talk every day might be thoroughly estranged.

The copersons who form awesome communities can be very different. The sense of community that matters in the ethics of awesomeness is one that can occur between people of different nationalities, classes, languages, and sexual preferences, for example. Creative community builders foster feelings of rapport among individuals, creating a sense of connection among us, often one that is inflected with joy, an expanded sense of self or world, or a deepened or refined sense of the richness and variety in the lives of individuals.

I argue in chapter 5 that awesomeness is, in a sense, an "American" phenomenon, in large part because of the promise of awesomeness to address sociocultural issues that arose in the United States in the past several decades.* But this doesn't mean awesomeness is restricted to the United States of America. Creative community building can happen in almost any culture or time, though in some it might not be very effective or much appreciated. (Sucking, by the way, is also a cross-cultural and historical phenomenon: Puritans basically made it a religious principle, and, well, North Korea exists.)

To appreciate the variety and breadth of creative community building, let's look at a range of examples. The examples show how many ways there are to institute awesomeness through creative community building. They also illustrate how being awesome is available to nearly anyone with insight, initiative, and courage—a truth that we will confirm several times over as we proceed, though we will also attend to the ways that class, privilege, social structures, power, and wealth can diminish

---

* Sarah Lyall hilariously brings out the Americanness of *awesome* by comparing US and British culture. See her essay "Ta-Ta, London. Hello, Awesome," *New York Times*, August 17, 2013.

access to creative community building and can change the dynamics of, and distort, the ethics of awesomeness.

Everyday Superman

The community that Fry's performance created was awesome but mostly fleeting (though he also brightened the days of millions of people who witnessed it through the Internet). The circumstance was special and the timing had to be just right. Others make creative community building a regular part of their lives.

When Auburn, Washington, resident Mark Wyzenbeek lost his wife in a car accident, he decided to change his life. His loss showed him that he should try to get as much out of each living day as he possibly could. Many people who feel this way resort to influential clichés about carpe diem, living in the moment, or "healthy lifestyles." Wyzenbeek, instead, wears a Superman costume nearly every day—one he made to absolute perfection himself. He wears it on airplanes, to bars, or just to walk around.

When people see Wyzenbeek in costume they respond with incredulity and excitement. They cannot resist commenting on and interacting with Superman. Wyzenbeek describes how people honk at him as they drive by: "The neat thing is, is when they honk at you. They're all looking and you hear this talk in the car like, 'Oh look there's Superman! There's Superman!' And the neat thing is, is they won't stop honking until you look at them. They have to have that eye contact with you, knowing that they're looking at you and that you *see* them looking at you, and then the whole cycle's complete and everyone's having a good time."*

That is awesome. Wyzenbeek's intrepid social presence breaks the norms and invites people to join him in the pretense that Superman is in town, getting gas or hanging at the local bar.

Mayor Antanas Mockus

Wyzenbeek's creative community building affected his local community, but some creative community builders operate in high office. It's one thing for your neighbor to wear a Superman costume in the spirit of awesomeness, but imagine if your mayor did.

Enter Antanas Mockus—a math and philosophy professor, former president of the National University of Colombia, two-time mayor of Bogotá, and very nearly the President of Colombia. Mockus, who had essentially no political experience, became the mayor of Bogotá in 1995 when it was one of the worst cities in the world, plagued by soaring pedestrian deaths caused by chaotic traffic; high rates of violent late-night fights and homicides; and a general collapse of civil respect and order. To ease the people's skepticism and hint at his leadership style, Mayor

---

* *This American Life*, episode 198, "How to Win Friends and Influence People," November 2, 2001.

Mockus wore a superhero costume with a large yellow *C* on the chest—it stood for "Super Citizen"—and walked the streets picking up garbage and inspiring people to do the same.

Mockus's creative community building brilliance goes far beyond this gesture. To address the serious traffic chaos and danger, he issued 350,000 thumbs-up and thumbs-down cards to be used by drivers. If a driver was not observing the rules, you could flash your thumbs-down card; if someone observed the rules, they would get a thumbs-up.

Mockus realized that Bogotans were more responsive to social stigma than to tickets or fines. The traffic police were notoriously corrupt, so Mockus replaced them with mimes, who ran around the city mocking people who littered, jaywalked, or violated traffic rules. The mimes would also praise people who did the right thing, creating mini-parades and scenes of joy. Mockus harnessed the power of creative community building by breaking the norms of public life and political rules: "People respond to humor and playfulness from politicians. It's the most powerful tool for change we have."*

Mockus-style play and humor is an especially powerful political tool where basic norms of civic rule and respect do not exist. Awesomeness can exist but cannot flourish in societies profoundly affected by violence, social injustice, or inequality. Peace, justice, and equality are the basic moral ingredients for

---

* Antanas Mockus, "The Art of Changing a City," *New York Times*, July 16, 2015.

an awesome culture. And hope for such a culture comes into sharper view as we progress toward a society where these basic ingredients are fully present (and blurs as we digress). Mockus had the insight to create moral, political, and civil motivation by juxtaposing the lack of these basic ingredients with the presence of awesomeness.

Mockus recognizes the communal character of his awesome leadership style: "There is a tendency to be dependent on individual leaders. To me, it is important to develop collective leadership. I don't like to get credit for all that we achieved. Millions of people contributed to the results that we achieved. . . . I like more egalitarian relationships."[*] To this end, he created social openings by simply asking people to join him in civic experiments. To address the late-night drunken fighting, homicides, and general danger of the city streets, Mockus instituted a "Night for Women." Men were asked to stay home and care for the family so that women, who were often stuck at home or just too afraid to go out into such a threatening city, could enjoy a night out for themselves. Policemen were also asked to step aside: Fifteen hundred policewomen provided the security for the night as seven hundred thousand women filled the bars and dance floors and brought a carnivalesque atmosphere to the streets. María Cristina Caballero reports, "In the lower-middle-

---

[*] María Cristina Caballero, "Academic Turns City into a Social Experiment," *Harvard Gazette*, March 11, 2004, http://news.harvard.edu/gazette/story/2004/03/academic-turns-city-into-a-social-experiment/.

class neighborhood of San Cristobal, women marched through the streets to celebrate their night. When they saw a man staying at home, carrying a baby, or taking care of children, the women stopped and applauded."*

Reconstructing the Street

You don't have to be the mayor of a major city to be an effective creative community builder. Cheap materials, artistic skill, creative insight, and courage can go a long way.

Tatyana Fazlalizadeh is a Brooklyn-based artist who was troubled by the way women are oppressed by harassing catcalls, solicitations, and generally unwelcome attention when simply walking down the street minding their own business. In a 2000 survey, 87 percent of women reported experiencing public harassment by men, and 30 percent reported being harassed on a regular basis.[†] A 2014 survey found that 65 percent of women report being harassed.[‡] This is not solely an urban phenomenon. Women who live in suburban (88 percent) or rural (90 percent) areas report slightly higher rates of harassment.[§] Such

---

* Ibid.

† "Oxygen/Markle Pulse Poll Finds: Harassment of Women on the Street Is Rampant; 87% of American Women Report Being Harassed on the Street by a Male Stranger," The Free Library, https://www.thefreelibrary.com/Oxygen/Markle Pulse Poll Finds: Harassment of Women on the Street Is . . . -a062870396.

‡ Holly Kearl, *Unsafe and Harassed in Public Spaces: A National Street Harassment Report* (Reston, VA: Stop Street Harassment, 2014).

§ "Oxygen/Markle Pulse Poll."

gender-based street harassment changes the character of public spaces for women, making it troubling, threatening, frustrating, and generally oppressive.

As Jane Jacobs writes in *The Death and Life of Great American Cities*, "The public peace—the sidewalk and street peace—of cities is not kept primarily by the police, necessary as police are. It is kept primarily by an intricate, almost unconscious network of voluntary controls and standards among the people themselves, and enforced by the people themselves."* But when this complex "network of voluntary controls and standards" is skewed toward the interests of a single group—say, heterosexual men— the street can become far less peaceful for people who aren't in that group.

Catcallers often report that they are merely appreciating women's beauty, when in fact they are threatening and diminishing it. Women who are harassed often feel timid, self-conscious, fearful, and uncomfortable—they do not feel like themselves as they walk down the street. By catcalling women, these men in fact erase whatever beauty is embodied in a prideful, comfortable, confident, or purposeful swagger. Even worse, they erase the beauty of a person simply being free to do whatever she wants, however she wants. In response to the harassment, many women change their behavior; 34 percent choose routes to avoid men who harass them and 32 percent avoid being alone

---

* Jane Jacobs, *The Death and Life of Great American Cities* (New York: Vintage Books, 1992), 31.

in public.* This also silences women's reasonable grievances against men who harass them—any direct verbal confrontation risks violent escalation.

Fazlalizadeh found an alternative way to dialogue with harassers and take issue with their distortion of public space. For her project *Stop Telling Women to Smile* she interviews women about their experiences of street harassment and asks them what they want to say. She draws their portraits and makes posters of them, along with a quote—for example, "Men do not own the streets"; "Women are not outside for your entertainment"; "My name is not baby"—and pastes them on the streets in highly visible public spaces.

Fazlalizadeh's creative intervention in public space gives women a voice against otherwise unreachable harassers. It shifts the network of controls and standards and allows women to reclaim the street as an egalitarian and communal public space. In doing so Fazlalizadeh institutes a more just public space, where people can pursue their personhood. But she also opens up a space where individuals can be themselves and awesomeness can emerge and thrive. Her posters not only depict individuals and place them in public—they give them an expressive voice in a space where they are otherwise forced into silence. And that is awesome. Fazlalizadeh is a creative community builder who uses street art to give women a voice and

* "Oxygen/Markle Pulse Poll."

restore their equal claim on public space, opening that space for them to be individuals in pursuit of individuality.

Turkish Jokes

Humor can also be used to establish an awesome creative interface between groups that would otherwise not interact much. And often there are significant barriers to interaction—like not speaking the same language or being from radically different cultures.

In 1994, the Dutch artist Jens Haaning went to the Turkish immigrant area of central Oslo, Norway. From a loudspeaker attached to a lamppost near a public square, Haaning broadcast various jokes and funny stories in Turkish, spoken by a native speaker. A similar project, *Turkish Mercedes*, occurred in Kreuzberg, a largely Turkish neighborhood of Berlin. Haaning broadcast Turkish jokes from a loudspeaker attached to the roof of a Mercedes-Benz with Turkish license plates.

The result was a crowd of initially puzzled Turkish people who looked around, and then at each other. They laughed together as they recognized a scattered group of Turkish speakers who understood the jokes. As French art critic and curator Nicolas Bourriaud writes, ". . . he produces in that split second a micro-community, one made up of immigrants brought together by collective laughter."* This work creates a social open-

---

* *Relational Aesthetics* (Dijon, France: Les Presses du Réel, 1998), 17.

ing for Turkish speakers who often feel marginalized in a foreign land. Haaning notes that the work created an unexpected second social opening: The square in Oslo became a meeting point of Filipino taxi drivers who felt more comfortable among other immigrants.*

But Haaning's work simultaneously creates a third, even more interesting social opening. By eliciting the mysterious collective laughter of immigrants in public, the work shifts the burden of social opening creation onto the in-power group—the native Norwegian or German speakers. This point is often missed in critical writing on these works that claim that the native Norwegian or German speakers are excluded. Art critic Jennifer Allen writes, "their laughter binds [the Turkish immigrants] while cutting them off from the native speaker in their adoptive countries who simply cannot understand why they are laughing." And Bourriaud writes that Haaning "injected a foreign language into the city's body, letting it bring together those who could speak it, thus for once excluding the 'natives,' leaving them without any ability to read the message."† What these remarks overlook is the fact that a loud collective laughter is a social opening for those who find it mysterious. Haaning creates a social opening for Turkish speakers and thereby creates a social opening between

---

* Reported in a talk titled "How Art Can Influence Politics and Vice Versa" given to the Swedish Exhibition Agency (2015).
† Both quotes are from Jens Haaning's catalog, "Hello, My Name Is Jens Haaning" (Dijon, France: Les Presses du Réel, 2002).

them and the dominant culture, whose members are given the opportunity to speak to the immigrants about what is going on. If they don't, then, well, you know.

•

These are just a few examples of exemplary creative community building—as we will see, there are many more. But our examples thus far show that creative community building comes in different shapes and sizes: It can be fleeting or long-lasting, bottom up or top down, fairly mundane or really profound, born of misery or in the spirit of fun, serious or lighthearted.

Bands, Booze, Art, and Shoes: Everything Is Awesome

The creative community builders canvassed in the previous section had awesome ideas, made awesome artifacts (costumes, art, props, collective action), and executed their ideas awesomely. That's a lot of awesomeness. So far we have developed a clear idea of what it means to say that a person's *action* is awesome or sucky. But what does it mean to say that a costume, a coffee shop, a social media app, street art, an idea, or a band is awesome? To quote from the song "Everything is Awesome!!!" by Canadian pop duo Tegan and Sara:

Blue skies, bouncy springs
We just named two awesome things
A Nobel prize, a piece of string
You know what's awesome? EVERYTHING!

But is it really true that everything is (or can be) awesome? Why do we associate awesomeness with *things*? The answer is that many, many things can be awesome or sucky—and this is an important fact about the ethics of awesomeness. To appreciate this fact, we will have to dwell briefly on a few more of the subtleties in the way we use the words *awesome* and *sucks*.

•

For starters, we should note that *awesome* and *sucks* are often used metaphorically, or nonliterally. Tom McCarthy's film *The Station Agent* contains a nice illustration of this. The three central characters—Finn (Peter Dinklage), Olivia (Patricia Clarkson), and Joe (Bobby Cannavale)—are sitting down to eat outside Joe's father's isolated roadside coffee stand. Joe's father is unwell, so Joe is looking after the stand. Finn is a quiet, somewhat reclusive man with dwarfism who is obsessed with trains and railroads. And Olivia is a sad and reflective woman who is separated from her husband after the death of their young son. In short, each character is isolated from the larger world. Olivia's isolation is due to pure and final misfortune. Finn's isolation is a part of his very identity, almost forced on him by the glares and taunts he receives as a dwarf. And Joe's isolation is out of duty to his father. Duty, cruelty, and misfortune—some of the most profound reasons we shut ourselves off from the world. Put them all together and you have an impromptu pork chop dinner on a dirty picnic table outside an old coffee stand along a rural New Jersey roadside.

Joe is by far the most gregarious of the three, and he's the chef and host, talking up his fried chops, beans, and rice. The meal is their first chance to emerge from their isolation and connect, if only to acknowledge each other's isolation. But as soon as Joe, with a giant grin on his face, serves everyone, he gets a phone call. He hangs up looking disappointed:

Joe: I gotta split.
Olivia: You're leaving?
Joe: Yeah, that was my dad. He can't find his medication. Totally sucks.

What, exactly, "totally sucks"? The context makes it clear that it's Joe's leaving the dinner. But according to our theory, Joe's leaving doesn't suck in the strict sense because he has a good reason to leave: His father, the reason he's running the coffee stand in the first place, needs help. Yet he's right to say that his leaving sucks because it sucks the life out of the rare social gathering. In other words, it's *as if* he's done something sucky. The effect and emotional resonance of his leaving is just like the effect and emotional resonance of true suckiness.

We use *awesome* and *sucks* like this often—when you miss the bus by a hair (sucks), step in poop (really sucks), or get a lucky break (pretty awesome).

Yet in other cases we use "awesome" and "sucks" literally in discussions of various cultural artifacts: from late-night snacks, restaurants, and novels to bands, booze, art, and shoes.

This broad literal usage can seem strange when we compare it to another couple of terms that we commonly use to evaluate and critique people and their actions: *moral* and *immoral*. These terms have had a seismic influence on our actions, thought, and speech. But unlike with *awesome* and *sucks*, it's a stretch to call various products of human culture "moral" or "immoral." It sounds odd, if not downright wrong, to say that a guitar or a drum machine is moral. But guitars and drum machines can definitely be awesome. It's a striking fact about the ethics of awesomeness that its central evaluative terms—*awesome* and *sucky*—apply so clearly and directly to both people and everyday things. Why is that?

Consider the character of our guiding ideal—the creative community builder. This isn't the image of a saint or a moral monk; it's not the ideal of a solo agent always acting on her very best reasons (even if she does), or of an ethical virtuoso always attuned to the highest good (even if she is). The ideal at the center of the ethics of awesomeness fuses a kind of ethico-aesthetic excellence with the aspiration for a *community* of *individuals*. Action in the ethics of awesomeness is always crew-oriented, or squad-minded, and is successful only if someone else takes up the social opening. Therefore, the awesome person—the creative community builder—must know what it takes to inspire *downness*. A person cannot be awesome unless someone else is down, game, chill, or awesome themselves. So the character traits, modes of responsiveness, and cultural tools and artifacts that inform the ethics of awesomeness are those that promote copersons and crews. The ultimate good in the ethics of awesomeness, then, is not some status that accrues to an individual, like moral virtuosity or sainthood. It's a positive state that takes two to institute, inherent in copersons and crews. Awesomeness essentially has others in mind—particularly other individuals.

It's for this reason that the ethics of awesomeness, unlike other ethical theories, is so attuned to various activities and products of human culture—to forms of play, cuisines, social media, coffee, bands, booze, art, and shoes. It's an ethics that is highly sensitive to activities, artifacts, and environments that facilitate awesomeness—Superman costumes, street art, pork chops, and drum machines. Or "awesome blossoms"—batshit giant fried onions that you can't eat alone (no judgment though).

Of course all of these things can be "good" or "cool" or whatever, but saying that they are *awesome* implicates them in a network of aspiring communal agents. It can be the focus of communal exploration, individual cultivation, and mutual appreciation. Saying that something *sucks* points out that it won't inspire downness—no one will be game to play a wack game, or up for chilling in a boring place. That game, that space—they suck the life out of things. When we say that an event, activity, or object is *awesome* we are hinting at its suitability for the ethics of awesomeness, for inspiring and sustaining creative community building.

Of course, we can relate to the culture of artifacts in better and worse ways when it comes to being awesome and not sucking. Being awesome is not a matter of simply buying the coolest things. To illustrate, consider the act of giving someone a gift. Gifting is generally awesome, but it is a complicated practice that takes many forms. If I make you an apple pie just for the hell of it, that's awesome. It's even more awesome if I use apples I grew or ones a coperson cultivated. But what if I just buy an apple pie from a supermarket or regift one that someone else made for me? What if I give you a McDonald's apple pie that I bought in a hurry because I knew I had to give you *something*? What if I give you a McDonald's apple pie that someone else bought in a hurry and gave to me?

What distinguishes these examples is the extent to which the act of gifting embodies the ethics of awesomeness. If I take the time to make something, perhaps riffing on a recipe I discovered, wrap it up beautifully, and thoughtfully give it to you—that's awesome. It expresses appreciable features of my sense of self and style. If I regift a cold McDonald's apple pie, it's almost as if I'm trolling you. Unless you really like them and I know it, my gift expresses almost nothing of interest—and that sucks.

An episode of *Seinfeld*, "The Deal" (season 2, episode 9), contains a funny illustration of this. Jerry gifts Elaine $182 cash:

> **Elaine:** You got me cash?
>
> **Jerry:** Well this way I figure you can go out and get yourself whatever you want. No good?
>
> **Elaine:** Who are you, my uncle?
>
> **Jerry:** Well come on. That's $182 right there. I don't think that's anything to sneeze at.
>
> **Elaine:** Let me see the card. [Reading] "To a wonderful girl, a great pal, and more." *Pal*? You think I'm your *pal*?
>
> **Jerry:** I said, "and more."
>
> **Elaine:** I am not your pal.
>
> **Jerry:** What's wrong with pal? Why is everyone so down on pal?

The problem with the gift, the card, and "pal" is that they suck. The gift does not express anything appreciable about Jerry, nor does it express any appreciation of Elaine's individuality, and Jerry recognizes this when he passes this interpretive, appreciative labor off onto Elaine: "I figure you can go out and get yourself whatever you want." The card is generic, and the term *pal* can be applied to pretty much anyone, including sworn enemies (*Step off, pal!*).

So listen, pal, what truth there is in the idea that "everything is awesome" comes down to this: Pretty much everything, given the right context, can be employed in the ethics of awesomeness as long as it plays a valuable role in the appreciation of individuality—even cold McDonald's apple pies. Maybe you and I have an inside joke about apple pies, or maybe our first date involved a cold McDonald's apple pie, or maybe I think cold McDonald's apple pies are really tasty. In these cases, even cold McDonald's apple pies can be awesome.

Living Together

The ethics of awesomeness is coming into view: It's an ethics that governs the expression and mutual appreciation of individuality; it looks to creative community builders for guidance and inspiration—people who use social creativity and various artifacts to inspire individuals to cultivate, explore, and express themselves. With this in view, we can begin to apply this way of thinking to a central ethical question, namely, the question of how to live together and treat each other, from our relationships and private interactions to civic life.

•

The psychologist John Gottman has been studying human relationships for decades. He wants to know what makes a human relationship healthy or unhealthy, and he has published his results in more than forty books. His research is so refined that in a 1992 study, he was able to predict with up to 94 percent accuracy whether a couple would divorce in the future.[*] One of Gottman's central discoveries is the importance of what he calls "bids for emotional connection." We make these bids to our partners, and we might do so by asking about their day, commenting on our shared environment, proposing a future plan, and so on. Gottman has observed in great detail how people react to their partner's bids. They might "turn toward" the bid in various ways, taking it up and engaging; they might "turn away" from the bid and deflect it; or they might "turn against" the bid and deflect and discourage it.[†] By now this should sound familiar. A bid is a type of social opening—one that specifically concerns emotional connection. If Gottman is right, then facility with the ethics of awesomeness is essential for healthy relationships.

Suppose you and your partner get in a huge fight. You want nothing to do with each other—you can barely look at each other, and you'd rather scream, cry, or storm out than battle for another millisecond. The ethics of awesomeness has some advice here: Inhale, hold it, exhale slowly, and proceed to be awesome.

---

[*] Buehlman, K., Gottman, J. M., and Katz, L. "How a Couple Views Their Past Predicts Their Future: Predicting Divorce from an Oral History Interview," *Journal of Family Psychology* 5, no. 3–4 (1992): 295–318.

[†] Gottman has many books and articles on these issues, but for an example see *The Science of Trust: Emotional Attunement for Couples* (New York: W.W. Norton and Company, 2011).

Preamble: *An epic fight somehow turns into an argument about fries.*

You: You know, this is just like last week when I *told you* I wanted calamari and you insisted on getting the fries!

Partner: Typical! We always have to do what *you* want to do. If I want fries then watch out. You're like some kind of preference dictator!

You [deep breath]: This sucks. What if we tried to make our own fries?!

Obviously that's a fake fight (I'll leave the real ones off the page). It's never easy, and sometimes it's not even possible, but creating a social opening in such situations can help both of you regroup and focus on what you appreciate about each other. When the time is right you can return to the topic of dispute, if it's even worth arguing about. Often you'll realize that it was a dumb thing to fight over in the first place. Being awesome in the middle of a fight can provide the needed respite and add character to a healthy connection.

The hit CBS sitcom *How I Met Your Mother* illustrates this. The longtime couple Marshall and Lily are awesome arguers (and advanced high-fivers, by the way). They have a rule that says that when they are in the middle of a fight either of them can "hit pause." This breaks the norms of arguing with your partner. Hitting pause means they have to immediately stop arguing; it allows them to forget about the fight for a moment and reconnect—and sometimes they *really* reconnect, if you catch my drift. When they hit "unpause" and resume the argument, they are usually in a much better place.

Of course, not all relationships are long term, and few are perfectly healthy. We have all known, perhaps all too personally, extremely one-sided friendships. One friend is always the one to invite the other over, include her in activities, or suggest fun things to do. The other friend always *takes up* the opportunities presented by her friend—she always comes over, hangs out, goes to dinner, grabs coffee, etc. She just never creates them herself. She's certainly not awesome, because she never *creates* social openings—so our theory can capture that. But some people would think that she also kind of sucks. How can we capture this thought, given that she never declines the social openings her friend offers? She seems down, even game—and never creating social openings oneself seems not to count as sucky in our theory.

Well, what are friendships? The term *friendship* covers an array of relationships—from long-term family-like connections to fairly short-term patterns of shared interests and time together. One thing friendships have in common, it seems, is that they all involve commitments to create social openings. In other words, to be in a friendship is to be more or less committed to being awesome toward your friend. If one friend never creates these opportunities, then it's as if she's invited you on a road trip—thereby suggesting that she'll do her share of the driving—

but isn't willing to drive. Which sucks. (As we will see in the next chapter, this "friend" is either being a "half-asser" or a "fake-ass person.")

To the extent that we are friends with *ourselves*, then, we are committed to giving ourselves such opportunities. One way to suck as a person is to suck toward yourself, to never give yourself such opportunities and to always enact the roles society expects you to enact. But we must be awesome to ourselves.

Sometimes being awesome to ourselves is a way of being awesome to others. Consider dating, in which love and romance are governed by strong cultural norms and powerful social roles. Wanna go on a date? How about the new restaurant downtown, dinner and a movie, kisses on the doorstep, discussing what you like, love, and hate, wine and flowers, sweet outfits, talk of family and life plans? We all know how to enact the generic role of person on a date.

You: Hi! So nice to see you again.

Date: You too! You look great.

You: Oh, thanks. Well so do you.

Date: So, my friend told me about this restaurant. Apparently we have to get the calamari.

You: My coworker ate here last week and said it was great. . . .

We all feel strong pressure to enact these roles when so much is at stake—this person could be "the one"; you want to make a good impression; you want them to make a good impression. But having the courage to be awesome can break up this routine and reveal your date's awesomeness or suckiness. Go to a café instead and make up stories about the people around you; hit up a bookstore and buy each other three books you think the other would like; do a late-night taste test of ten items at Jack in the Box (emphasis on *taste*) and discuss your culinary findings. OK, maybe that's stuff I would want to do, but you can think of your own awesome date ideas.

> **You:** Hi! So nice to see you again.
> **Date:** You too! You look great.
> **You:** Oh, thanks. Well, so do you.
> **Date:** So, my friend told me about this restaurant. Apparently we have to get the calamari.
> **You:** That sounds good, but what if we [INSERT AWESOMENESS]?

Your date can take up your social opening or bat it down. We can imagine an "Oh yeah, I'm game!" response, or a kinda sucky "Well, I really *would* like to try the calamari . . ." response. But Awesomeness > Calamari. If your date doesn't realize that, then it might be a sign.*

When I moved from Berkeley, California, to New York City

---

* There's actually a website for awesome dates called HowAboutWe, where people post their awesome date ideas and try to find a good match.

in 2007 I quickly realized that really good Mexican food was nowhere to be found. I would have been perfectly happy eating tacos and burritos all day, every day, so this was going to be a problem. When I started dating a cute redhead who seemed to know every cool restaurant in Brooklyn, I wasted no time telling her about my longing. On our second or third date, she showed up with the most perfect, fresh, delicious handmade tortillas I had ever seen. And this is a person who will argue at length that pizza is superior to burritos. In spite of that, she is awesome. We got married and now live in San Diego, surrounded by some of the world's best tortillas.

Social openings intervene in our roles, habits, and norms, and as we have noted, there are several strategies one can use to intervene. Depending on the situation, we might use jokes, gifts, friendly gestures, displays of talent, and style, among other things. However, there are social roles that are defined so as to make any such intervention inappropriate. This makes sense in some cases—we probably shouldn't joke around too much with a federal judge who is considering the legality of our actions. But certain cultures and social roles are inherently sucky because they rule out any such intervention for no good reason. This is vivid among people who adhere to rigid stereotypes and reinforce the stereotypes of others. It's even more vivid in socially stratified societies with pronounced socioeconomic disparities, wherein people of "lower" status, class, or means cannot so much as speak to those of "higher" status, class, or means. The higher, elite, or privileged roles are usually inhabited by very sucky people. They're too important, educated, rich, or consequential for the unimpressive, dumb, oppressed, poor, or unlucky folks. Any role or type of person in general that categorically disallows or prevents social openings with entire groups of people is highly sucky. The ethics of awesomeness encourages social openings with all kinds of people and walks of life.

One type of person who can seem to think he's too important is the *wayward citizen*—the litterer, the tailgater, the noisy straphanger. We think these people suck, but why? On the face of it, they haven't been presented with a social opening. They're just going about their business, or lack thereof, and sucking. Furthermore, by littering or tailgating they're disrupting a range of "ordinary public reasons," entrenched social habits, and civic norms—norms we follow to make living together more efficient, safe, and clean.

Seinfeld's George Costanza suggests an answer. He insists that we understand that we live together in a society, and we have tacitly agreed on a range of reasonable rules and conventions that keep the community intact—including rules about where and how to stand on the subway, walk down the sidewalk, sit at a bus stop, or ask for the time or for samples of ice cream.* They aren't just habits or rules; they are habits and rules

---

* Another example is season 6, episode 3 of Larry David's *Curb Your Enthusiasm*—a show full of examples of people sucking. Larry David's character is fascinating in part because he

of respectful community—the kind of basic community we need in order to be awesome. When George Costanza sees someone breaking those rules—particularly when, and perhaps *only* when, it negatively affects him, but we'll ignore that—he lets them know by yelling, "You know, we live in a society!"

The contrast to living in a society is living alone, and George is reminding people that we don't in fact live alone. We live together, and we have these rules for a reason—we keep them in place to keep each other together as a community. We need to maintain a background of just and useful social norms against which our individuality can be expressed, understood, and appreciated. These are the background norms that make awesomeness possible. By ignoring and acting against them, the wayward citizen suggests that awesomeness doesn't matter. And he thereby sucks.

But, as we have seen, sometimes those norms are unjust or otherwise unacceptable, and we can use creative strategies to disrupt them in an awesome way, as with Fazlalizadeh's street art and Mockus's artistic civic interventions. A society's potential for awesomeness depends on the forms of public and social life it constructs and sustains. The most extreme examples are rigidly hierarchical societies—for example, ones structured by strict rules of class, wherein higher- and lower-class people cannot interact—or deeply sexist or segregated societies.

---

obsessively calls attention to sucky people while being no stranger to suckiness. Consider his arguably sucky attitude toward the "stop and chat."

To appreciate the ways social norms and roles can interfere with awesomeness, let's travel back in time again to consider how the coffee shop conversation might go in Montgomery, Alabama, in 1953:

> **Employee:** Hi there, darlin', what can I do for you today?
> **You:** I would like a large coffee, please.
> **Employee:** All right, that'll be ten cents, please.
> **You:** Small price to become human again. Here you go.
> **Employee:** [???]

What comes next? The answer depends entirely on who you are and how you look. Are you male or female? Black or white? Gay or straight? Able-bodied or not? What comes next also depends on whether there are norms dictating *how* you can appear—what you can wear, how you can sound and seem. Does your hair match stereotypes that apply to your sex, your race, your class? If you are black, are you even allowed inside the restaurant? Can you even express what you would like? In many cases, the employee wouldn't address you in the first place. If you are female, then there might be a question about why you are in public without a man at your side, or why you are drinking such a "manly" drink. "Oh," the employee might say, "I didn't think you'd be drinking this all by your little self!" Of course, if you are an "appropriately" dressed, able-bodied white male speaking English without an outsider's accent, then maybe, just maybe you can try to create a social opening.

There can be serious obstacles to awesomeness written directly into norms of interaction. These obstacles come from sucky attitudes about sex, race, class, gender, and sexual orientation, among other prejudices and biases that restrict our ability to appreciate, explore, or express individuality. They tell people which kinds of individuals they can and cannot appreciate, or they place barriers on which kinds of people can express themselves or, if they can, how they must do it. The ethics of awesomeness celebrates the cultivation, expression, exploration, and appreciation of individuality. Other things being equal, any norms that suppress, discourage, rule out, or inhibit such expression suck.

Another way social norms and roles can conflict with the ethics of awesomeness is if they include or promote features of individuality that not everyone shares. Some pernicious, unjust, or immoral social norms tell us to be certain kinds of individuals, and in doing so they can obscure genuine expressions of individuality and harm the people we interact with.

We see an example of this in *Sex and the City*, season 1, episode 11, "The Drought." Miranda has hit a dry spell in her sex life and is yearning for change, but one evening she finds herself (yet again) without a date or any social plans. On her way into a video store for a movie rental and some gummy bears, a construction worker hollers at her:

Man: Hey, hey! It's my sweetheart! You're lookin' good, baby, good enough to eat. Where you goin', doll? I got what you want. I got what you need.

Miranda: You talkin' to me?

Man: Oh, we got a live one, boys!

Miranda: You got what I want? You got what I need?

Man: Uh-huh.

Miranda: Well what I want is to get laid. What I *need* is to get laid. *I need to get laid.*

Man: Take it easy, lady. I'm married.

Miranda: All talk and no action, huh? What a *gavone* [pig]!*

Here the man is enacting the role of the urban construction worker, who, in addition to building things, gives himself the privilege of being extremely personal with any and all women who pass by, harassing them with taunts and claims of sexual mastery, presenting himself as a "dirty Don Juan." But for the construction worker, enacting this role makes him a fake-ass person—he's married, doesn't want to damage his marriage, and really has no interest in Miranda.

Society needs construction workers, and the role of construction worker must include various good qualities related to

---

* For a real-world example of a woman who decided to treat catcalls as legitimate social openings in order to flip the script and question the catcallers' beliefs and motivations, listen to philosopher Eleanor Gordon-Smith's piece "Hollaback Girl" on *This American Life*, episode 603, "Once More, with Feeling," December 2, 2016.

the practical tasks of building: One must be reliable, a team player, physically quite strong and resilient. But one doesn't need the extraneous feature of dirty Don Juan. When it's included, all construction workers are scripted to act that way whether or not they have fervid libidos and loud mouths.

Or whether they even like women. In the Netflix comedy series *Unbreakable Kimmy Schmidt*, Kimmy has recently moved to NYC after escaping from an underground bunker, where she was held against her will for years by a doomsday cult leader and religious fanatic. She's entirely naive about the ways of the world, so when a construction worker catcalls her, she doesn't know what it means:

Man: Hey Red, you're making me wish I was those jeans.

Kimmy: Well I wish I was your yellow hat.

Man: What?

Kimmy: It's my favorite color. . . . Did I say something wrong?

Man: All right, I'm sorry about the jeans thing. You made your point.

Kimmy: And my point is . . . ?

Man: That I say these things to women even though I got a mother that I love, and three beautiful sisters. OK? Are you happy?

Kimmy: Happy, but nervous. My friend from Indiana is coming to visit.

Man: Why do I talk to women like that? What are we doing here guys—I mean, big picture? Does the world really
need another bank?

Later in the episode we encounter the construction worker
again. He's been reflecting on his attitudes toward women and
has come to accept that he's gay. In season 2 (episode 2) we
encounter him again and he explains that he can't really be himself at work; he has to "put up a front" on the job and act like
he's into women.

These examples suggest that good social norms, according
to the ethics of awesomeness, are those that are *generic* in a
sense: They don't tell us how to express our individuality; they
don't tell us what kinds of copeeps we can have or what kinds
of individuals we can be or appreciate. Good social norms allow the ethics of awesomeness to flourish. As long as we are
being respectful, they don't tell us how we must present ourselves; they don't bleed into our individuality in a way that
makes it unclear whether we are merely enacting a role or actually expressing our individuality. For a painter to make a painting, she needs a good blank canvas. It would suck if every
painter who wanted to paint had to use a canvas that already
had a bright red square on it. Good interpersonal norms derive
from the clear canvas of personhood; they depend primarily
on capacities and sentiments we all share or all rightly demand
of one another—our capacities for respect, trust, and equal

consideration (to name a few). In other words, good interpersonal norms are such that, when we are not being awesome or sucky, we are perfectly polite by merely following the script, no matter who we are or who we are interacting with. Such norms are the best rules to riff on and break—the rich and reliable soil of social life in which the inter-individual norms of awesomeness can grow and blossom.

Introverts and Expectations

Even when social norms are acceptable and aren't obstructing awesomeness, there can be personal obstacles to the kind of social engagement that the ethics of awesomeness governs. Some people generally avoid hanging out and seeking social connection. Too much socializing often saps their energy, so even if they like to, they cannot hang very long. The introverts among us are wary of forced togetherness and are hesitant to take up social openings, especially when it might mean a prolonged encounter or a lot of small talk. And when they do take them up, they don't always do it very well. This might suggest that introverts are among the suckiest of all, but they aren't.

The reason they aren't sucky is that introverts often have some of the best reasons to opt out of social openings—from the casual chatty workplace conversation to the raucous party. They report that they need a lot of time alone to gather the social strength that is all too easily sapped by social interaction. As a result, introverts might *seem* to suck because they're always ducking out, barely engaging, deflecting attempts at conversation. But they really do need the time alone, and they really are inordinately affected by too much social interaction. They don't suck because they have good reasons to act as they do and to opt out of social openings that non-introverts might readily accept.

As a result, introverts have the unenviable task of having to manage the sucky image that can develop in the eyes of their non-introverted peers. The impression they might leave on these peers is often one they have to deflect or correct. Extroverts face a similar problem at the other end of the spectrum. They are not automatically awesome—they have to be careful to not let their enthusiasm for socializing transform into sucky forms of over-performance: thunder stealing or self-promoting. The ethics of awesomeness cuts across the introvert-extrovert divide. "Awesome extrovert" is not redundant, and "awesome introvert" is certainly not an oxymoron, though it may be a challenge.

The challenge can be met in numerous ways. As we saw with Fazlalizadeh's and Haaning's artworks, creating social openings—and being awesome in general—does not require face-to-face interaction. We can create social openings with thoughtful gestures like leaving gifts and notes for people or sending them in the mail, making and delivering food, or writing a story, song, or poem. The British artist Georgina Starr created a performance called *Dining Alone*, in which she invited people who were dining solo in a Parisian restaurant to visit the wine cellar, where they could dine by candlelight and listen to her reflections on her own experience dining alone.* This social opening creates an empathetic connection about the particulars of the experience of dining alone but does not require socializing or face-to-face interaction.† We can all tap into the spirit of awesomeness, and we can all partake of the joys of creative community building, introverts and extroverts alike.

But we have to know our limits and not expect too much from ourselves or each other. When it comes to being awesome and not sucking, we have to make sure we have fair and just expectations of people. Our expectations for introverts cannot be the same as they are for extroverts and run-of-the-mill social folk. Distorted expectations can result from indefensible ideas about ability, race, gender, class, and so on. As we will discuss later when we talk about the origins of awesome, there is a shameful history of white people expecting black entertainers to take up any social openings they proposed, no matter how insensitive or absurd. And as Fazlalizadeh's street art reveals, the expectations for women to accept social openings can be so severe as to be socially crippling. These things are not only deeply immoral and unjust, they also really suck. A truly

---

* The text she read is available here: http://georginastarr.com/georginastarrdiningalone.htm.
† Note that I'm not saying this kind of interaction will appeal to all introverts. However, because such a social opening does not require much face-to-face interaction, it might be taken up by, or inspiring to, someone who would rather avoid such interaction.

awesome society and culture is one whose expectations are fair and equal across race, gender, and sexual orientation—and it's one that is sensitive to people's differing approaches to flourishing in the ethics of awesomeness.

•

But what exactly are these different approaches? We now have before us the outlines of the ethics of awesomeness. Sucking is a matter of failing to take up social openings; not sucking is a matter of taking them up and engaging; and being awesome is a matter of creating them. The ethics of awesomeness concerns the ways of being and responding to creative community builders, who give us models, ideas, and motivation for awesomeness, and whose creation or deployment of cultural artifacts—bands, booze, art, and shoes—provides a locus for the cultivation and mutual appreciation of individuality. This way of thinking illuminates why we regard such a wide variety of things as awesome or sucky, from unicycles and barbecues to bad friends and wayward citizens.

But so far we have mapped the mere surface of the ethics of awesomeness. Now we must wield philosophy's steel shovel and dig deep into the many ways of engaging in the ethics of awesomeness—from being down, game, and chill to being a thunder stealer, douchebag, or fake-ass person.

Chapter 4

Mapping the Ethics of Awesomeness

PEOPLE WHO ARE game don't suck, but killjoys and blow-hards do. Why is that? What's the difference between being game and being down? How is a killjoy different from a stick-in-the-mud? And why do they both suck? In this chapter, we explore how the theory of suckiness and awesomeness provides a systematic answer to these questions by revealing a deep connection between concepts like being a blowhard, self-promoter, or killjoy and being game, chill, or down.

Our inquiry here will add to the ethics of awesomeness an account of the dynamics of participation in social openings, which are complex and often unpredictable affairs—a fact we are in danger of overlooking if we focus too much on creative community builders and not enough on those who respond to and take up social openings. Our investigation in this chapter will

reveal a systematic connection between awesomeness and suckiness, and a range of ways that people can be awesome or not.

As Norman Mailer tells us, "It is impossible to conceive a
new philosophy until one creates a new language, but a new
popular language . . . does not necessarily present its philosophy
overtly."* In thinking through the contemporary meanings of
the popular words *sucks* and *awesome*, we have begun to construct a picture of a new philosophy that many will recognize
and some will even identify with. As Mailer suggests, if we
want to understand this philosophy in more detail, we should
understand the nuances of the language that it's bound up with.
It is also important to look beyond *sucks* and *awesome* and appreciate how much the ethics of awesomeness has shaped our collective tongue. As Iris Murdoch warns, if we remain at the level
of *sucks* and *awesome* we risk impoverishing our understanding
of ethical nuance and being blind to some of the subtler ways
the ethics of awesomeness operates. We must discuss the subtle
and separate virtues and vices in the ethics of awesomeness.†

As we will see in this chapter, the language of the ethics of
awesomeness is not impoverished at all—it's a language we

---

* He says this in his 1957 essay on the meaning of *hip*, "The White Negro."
† "It is a shortcoming of much contemporary moral philosophy that it eschews discussion
of the separate virtues, preferring to proceed directly to some sovereign concept such as
sincerity, or authenticity, or freedom, thereby imposing, it seems to me, an unexamined and
empty idea of unity, and impoverishing our moral language in an important area." (*The
Sovereignty of Good*, 56.) Murdoch wrote this in the 1960s, and moral philosophy since has
been much better about investigating the "separate virtues," but it is advice well worth
keeping in mind.

share, part of our distinctive form of life, but one whose interstices and interconnections we don't yet grasp. One of the strengths of our way of thinking about awesomeness is its ability to systematize our understanding of these terms and thereby of the nuanced dynamics of social openings.

The Taxonomy of Suckiness and Awesomeness (pp. x–xi) will be our guide as we sweep across it from left to right. The professor in me will take charge of the discussion as we categorize, taxonomize, and evaluate our way through the intricacies of awesomeness and suckiness. The diagram is structured by our concept of a social opening and the different ways a person can relate to one: You can either opt out, opt in, be a nonstarter, take one up, or create one. Along the way, I'll suggest strategies for managing suckiness and will note various ways we can motivate awesomeness and non-suckiness in ourselves and others.

The Taxonomy of Suckiness and Awesomeness does not exhaust all the ways we have of talking about these matters; in fact, it's just a start. But it's a good start. I'll periodically suggest ways of expanding it.

Modes of Suckiness

Let's start on the left-hand side of the diagram, where we have a supercell of suckiness. There are three general ways to suck. The most basic is to opt out of a social opening for no good reason. Another way to suck is to opt in and let down. Many social openings are lengthy and dynamic—we might opt in to an extended social opening but fail to handle it well. The third way to suck is to be a "nonstarter"—someone who, in one way or another, is fundamentally against taking up social openings.

One note before we get started. You might be wondering why we have so many more words for ways of sucking than we do for ways of not sucking. While it's important to have ways of encouraging people to keep breathing life into the social activity, a social opening is a delicate thing and we have to be sensitive to actions that threaten to suffocate it. Many of these concepts are useful in understanding what went wrong with a social opening, but they also help us act well when we are in the middle of lengthy or dynamic social openings, keeping them alive and well.

Opting Out

As we discussed in detail in chapter 2, we suck when we opt out of a social opening for no good reason. This is the most basic way to suck, but there are in fact two ways to do this: by being simply sucky and by being wack.

Simply Sucky

Being *simply sucky* is the basic case of suckiness: We encounter a social opening and fail to take it up. When we say we would love to catch up but cancel at the last minute on a whim; when we say we'll come to the party but just decide not to and don't tell anyone; when we never accept our colleague's invitations to dinner, drinks, or the movies; when we go to an event we know our friend would love but don't invite them or tell them about it—these actions simply suck.

Many people would say that anyone who acts this way is being "lame," but I want to say something about the contemporary use of this word. Historically, the word *lame* was widely used to refer to people and animals (especially horses) who have difficulty walking. When it initially found use as a term of social criticism, it was used as a metaphor to describe people who lack effort, are dull, or are uninspired—that is, its use derived from the idea that such people are acting as if they are unable to walk. This usage has been the subject of understandable criticism because it seems to suggest or presume that being unable to walk is inherently bad or inferior, which is patently false and indeed offensive to people with disabilities and anyone who cannot walk or cannot do so in the species-normal way.

My linguistic sense says that nowadays *lame*, like *sucks*, has, in mainstream usage, shed this past and gained a new meaning. The metaphor has arguably died, giving *lame* a new literal meaning, which in common parlance has nothing to do with physical ability—it refers directly to a kind of social ineptitude, lack of spirit or effort, or social dullness. That said, people may be understandably offended by the term, and so it should be used, if at all, with caution, disavowal, or only when the social meaning is clear. As it is, the word is commonly used to pick out a widespread and culturally significant social attitude or disposition, and it's not clear that there is another word we can use instead (the words *dull*, *spiritless*, *disengaged*, and *bland* are . . . dull, spiritless, disengaged, and bland alternatives). Our theory suggests that the best alternative to *lame* is *simply sucky*; instead of "That's lame" we can say, "That simply sucks," or "That just [merely] sucks," so that's what you'll find here.

Management: If someone is being simply sucky, then they think they have a good reason not to take up a social opening, but they don't. There are two strategies you can employ. First, you might attempt to convince them that their reason for opting out is no good. This is a somewhat risky strategy because they think their reason is good; by trying to convince them otherwise you are in danger of pressuring them or seeming insensitive to their way of thinking and entrenching them in their suckiness. The second strategy avoids this result: You might encourage them to be down by convincing them that the value of being down is greater than the value of opting out for whatever reason they have. In other words, instead of suggesting that they have a bad reason, see if you can show that their reason isn't as good. Try to make vivid the thought that being down is better than their reason for opting out.

This applies to self-criticism too. If you're inclined to opt out, then introspect and ask yourself why you're disinclined. Pay attention to the voice that is afraid of the unfamiliar, scared of the uncertain, or wary of the new. That voice is often habitual, reactive, and simply sucky. Closer inspection and careful reflection might reveal a legitimate reason to opt out—and so to avoid suckiness—or you might revive your connection to the value of being up. You might even activate the spirit of awesomeness.

WACK

Some people take suckiness to another level. They not only refuse the social opening for no good reason, they actively disparage it—they decline while casting aspersions or implying that they're above it. It's unclear whether colloquial English contains a term for such actions and people. My suggestion is that we call them *wack*.

Wack people not only decline social openings, but are actively or symbolically against them for no good reason. They opt out while criticizing or dismissing, perhaps implicitly, the activity, or implying that they're better than or above it. It's one thing to opt out of a social opening—quite another to do so while flagrantly criticizing it or the people who create it.*

The reason it makes sense to say such a person is being "wack" can be illustrated by considering the fact that wackness is also

---

* Of course, some attempts at creating social openings merit criticism because they are discriminatory, unjust, presumptuous, harmful, and so on. In that case, we have good reason to criticize and deflect.

(and was originally) a feature of a person's style, the way they express their individuality in their decisions and actions—the way they dance, dress, walk, sing, rap, and so on. The person with wack style is someone whose style seems to openly flout the values and standards that define a thriving culture or activity. Case in point: President Obama was once criticized for the "wack-ass" tan suit he wore instead of his usual gray or navy.* The wackness of the mullet hairstyle, for another example, consists in its being so blatantly out of touch—so magnificently alien, given certain values—that the most aggressive ones seem almost to don a halo of confused confidence. The mullet effectively says, "I don't care about your party—mine's better." What wack people have in common with people who have wack style is that they both seem to flaunt a disregard for certain values the appreciation of which plays an essential role in a healthy social opening.

Management: When someone is being wack, we can try to reason with them, like we do with the simply sucky. But wack people wield a special and often mysterious opposition and even animosity that can be difficult to diagnose on the spot, and you may have to resort to other tactics to let people know that they are being sucky. If you're feeling bold, then you might try to wack back, giving the person a little taste of their own medicine. They might not come around, but at least they'll have

---

* Caity Weaver, "President Obama Shames America by Wearing Wack-Ass Tan Suit," *Gawker*, August 28, 2014, http://gawker.com/president-obama-shames-america-by-wearing-wack-ass-tan-1628136603. I'm down with the tan suit.

something to reflect on. Or you might just need to leave wack people to their own devices and hope they come to see the good in the social openings they mistakenly disparage. In other words, being chill in the face of wackness is often our only recourse. It can create a stark contrast and accentuate the wack features of a wack persona or move. We can only hope they see the good in our chillness and learn from their own mistakes.

Opting In and Letting Down

Being simply sucky or wack are not the only ways to suck—but they are the main ways of sucking that concern opting out of social openings. Among those who initially take up these opportunities—who opt in—there are many who suck. In fact, this is where suckiness really chafes. People who are simply sucky or wack thankfully opt out before the social opening really expands, but some people effectively opt out in the middle of it, holding out a promise of awesomeness without fully delivering. I call these people *killjoys*. Since social openings are complex and dynamic, there are many ways of being a killjoy. They divide into ways of underperforming, being a bore, and overperforming.

UNDERPERFORMING KILLJOYS (OR STICKS-IN-THE-MUD)

A standard type of underperforming killjoy is the *stick-in-the-mud*. This person takes up the social opening but, in one way or another, doesn't fully commit or succeed; everyone else is participating, talking, playing, dancing, or whatever, and they're stuck there. But there are several ways to be "stuck;" thus, there are several versions of the stick-in-the-mud: Consider the half-asser, the preference dictator, and the cheapskate.

Half-Assers

Half-assers present themselves as being down or game but then they don't put much effort into the activity. They aren't really present or engaged; they use scripted responses and rely on various heuristics, stereotypes, and habits. People who are always "merely polite" are often half-assers—they take up the social opening but fail to present their individuality and hide it behind a facade of respect. That's a decent and understandable response to brief or one-off social openings, but not always in a more extended and dynamic context. Half-assers seem to understand the value of not sucking but lack the insight or motivation, or haven't developed the skills, to thrive.

Management: Half-assers are probably trying to be minimally up or chill but can't muster the motivation or don't wield the requisite insight. That's fine, but it puts you in the position of picking up the slack (being the other ass cheek?). Use your downness to lead by example. Of course, that might not work. Sometimes you just have to let a half-asser off the hook. Let them be and don't allow their half-assery to diminish the overall awesome.

Preference Dictators

Another type of underperforming killjoy has very strict and inflexible ideas about how to carry out the social openings they take up. These people are on the dance floor, so to speak, but they're telling everyone how to dance. I like to call them *preference dictators*: They seem to understand the value of coperson-hood but think it consists of everyone meeting *their* preferences. They engage in social openings only when things are going their preference-dictating way.

This occurs commonly with dietary preferences and food fads. Sir Roger Scruton has a characteristically cutting, though overstated, description of the food-preference dictator:

> The rudeness of the glutton and the face stuffer are obvious. Equally ill-mannered—though it is politically incorrect to say so—is the food faddist, who makes a point of announcing, wherever he goes, that just this or this can pass his lips, and all other things must be rejected, even when offered as a gift. . . . [V]egetarians and vegans have now succeeded in policing the dinner table with their non-negotiable demands, ensuring that even when invited into company, they sit down alone.*

Scruton is wrong to think that all vegans and vegetarians are preference dictators. Most vegans and vegetarians do not have

---

* Roger Scruton, "Real Men Have Manners," in *Philosophy of Food*, ed. David M. Kaplan (Berkeley: University of California Press, 2012).

"nonnegotiable" demands. In fact, they have decent reasons for not eating meat and are willing to share those reasons. The question in any given context will be how they express those reasons, and whether the value of forcefully expressing them outweighs the awesomeness that a social opening around food can cultivate. The truly sucky food-preference dictator cannot let their decisions go unnoticed, draw excessive attention to their moral position, and persistently let their food values determine the character of their social interactions. This is true of many people who have various life-orienting commitments—from Paleo dieters and picky eaters to exercise fanatics and music snobs. There's nothing sucky about having such commitments, but there are more and less sucky ways of bringing them into play in an awesome social opening.

Preference dictators have appreciable values—worthy perspectives on food consumption and farming practices, exercise, health choices, lifestyle, art, and so on. But the true preference dictator's actions are rigidly and loudly governed by these values—ones that are indeed a matter of individuality and relevant to the social opening but not in the way imagined by the preference dictator. By making or suggesting that everyone conform to a certain set of preferences, the preference dictator ensures that those who have different preferences cannot comfortably express them. To that extent they cannot present themselves for appreciation—their love, insight, knowledge, and passion with respect to those preferences is muted. And when a large part of a person is muted in this way, it all too easily affects the rest of the person. Her attention and efforts are aimed at conforming to the will of the preference dictator, and she can't just be herself. In this way, the preference dictator spawns underperformance. In that sense, then, Scruton is on to something when he writes that preference dictators "sit down alone"; they sit down with diminished copeople.

Management: The preference dictator should chill a bit. The best tool here is direct confrontation. The preference dictator should know that their values are appreciated but that it is not chill, and definitely not awesome, to project in behavior, tone, and voice that everyone else should have the same ones. Remind the preference dictator that other people have their own views about food, lifestyle, art, and so on. Shift the focus and suggest that perhaps this is an opportunity to explore new music, discuss a social or political issue, or engage in a new activity. Social openings are opportunities for expression, exploration, and appreciation, not opportunities for extended sanctimony, preaching, judgment, or propagandizing.

If you find yourself with preference-dictating inclinations, consider an awesome approach to conveying the worth of your values and attitudes: Speak your piece and then let the social opening breathe a bit. Instead of preference dictating, invite your potential coperson over for a meal that embodies your food values, suggest a film or documentary that conveys the value of your social or political views, or tell a story that reveals why you love the things you love so much.

Cheapskates

Perhaps Scruton is confusing the preference dictator with the control freak (and its various subspecies, e.g., micromanagers and such). Control freaks have an unshakable urge to take charge, manage, or ensure that things are done precisely as they see fit. Perhaps they act out of a fear of unpredictability, or an irrational sense that only they can get things right. Control freaks suck, for sure, but their control-freakish preferences and values are not appreciable features of individuality. Another type of killjoy who exhibits preference-dictating tendencies, but who isn't a preference dictator, is someone who imposes their values in a dominating way but those values are not features of individuality—so the values they express and impose are irrelevant to the social opening.

To make this category clear, let's focus on the *cheapskate*, who's generally inclined to take up social openings and play along just like anyone else, until money enters the picture. Then everything changes. Their behavior becomes wholly regulated by the overarching norm that tells them to avoid spending more money than absolutely necessary. Preference dictators have rigid preferences that are relevant to the social opening; their preferences constitute aspects of individuality that are appropriately expressed in the context of awesomeness. Cheap-skates, however, have dominant and irrelevant preferences that make them unreceptive to the dynamics of the social opening; they have an excessive concern with money—one that suckily overshadows the expressive concerns of being awesome and not sucking. The other person always has to drive; they care not about the good beer but the cheap beer; you categorically must go to the movies on Tightwad Tuesday.

Cheapskates are people whose behavior is dominated by a value that is irrelevant to the social opening. It's not about be-ing broke—you can be broke and awesome at the same time—it's about overvaluing the saving of money at the expense of awesomeness. Instead of focusing on the conversation, the cheapskate is busy noting how much everything costs, forget-ting to do things for or accommodate others. Some people take cheapskatery to such an extreme that it runs their entire life: They try to get everything for free, measure out tap water with tablespoons, ask fellow diners for their uneaten food, or pick up every valuable item they find, including garbage they imagine repurposing as toilet paper or kitchen supplies.

The pursuit of cheapness or a good deal can be awesome: the underappreciated food joint, the great thrift shop, the stuffed carpool on a camping trip. In some circumstances, the goal of saving money can create an awesome social opening. Doing so can inspire action so fascinating and novel that it creates social openings. This is basically what happens in an episode of

TLC's disturbing show *Extreme Cheapskates*.* Jordan Mederich, who calls himself an "extreme barterer," enthusiastically recites Lewis Carroll's *Jabberwocky* in exchange for a raspberry doughnut in a doughnut shop. He then teaches his friend Jonathan to use his opera singing skills to get a deal on a cake for his wedding. Jonathan walks into a cake shop, approaches the baker, and offers to sing the aria "Nessun Dorma" from Puccini's opera *Turandot*. It turns out that the baker loves opera ("except Wagner") and applauds Jonathan's performance. He gets a discount on his wedding cake and the baker enjoys some operatic singing.

People like Jordan Mederich seem to really love bartering and, for that reason, either aren't really cheapskates or are a very unusual kind. The true cheapskate ventures far from awesomeness. When they are out to a nice meal with friends they say they "aren't that hungry" and then scarf cold pizza when they get home. Or they order an appetizer and eat all the free bread. Or, when the bill comes, they try to underpay by playing dumb or pretending they didn't eat any of the fries.

Management: Try playing on the cheapskate's turf—create social openings that are cheap, or that don't involve money. When your social openings do involve money, you might try to finesse that part of the social opening—arrange for the bill to be divided, deal with money in advance, or, if you can, just be gen-

---

* http://www.tlc.com/tv-shows/extreme-cheapskates/.

erous and pay for your coperson. These strategies will help the cheapskate focus and be reminded that often it doesn't really matter if someone else paid two dollars less than you.

If you find yourself with cheapskate tendencies, get creative. Maybe you can practice bartering. Instead of eating all the fries and pretending you aren't hungry, suggest splitting something with a coperson. Instead of going to the movies, invite some friends over, dust off an oldie but goodie, or hunt for a cheap treasure at a thrift store.

In other, more general, words, try to transform your irrelevant preferences into relevant ones. By splitting a meal you're sharing; by seeking alternative movies to watch, you're jointly expanding your film knowledge and appreciation; and so on. The same advice applies to other forms of dominant but irrelevant value expression, like being controlling or micromanaging.

Bores

There is a vexing category between under- and overperformers. *Bores* take up the social opening and at least ostensibly put in effort, but their efforts are in vain. Their general engagement isn't scripted or rote—it's just boring or spiritless. Their stories fall flat, their jokes are met with silence, their style doesn't inspire. In other words, they have a minimal understanding of how not to suck, but they haven't developed various virtues of awesomeness that allow them to flourish. They suck because they present features of individuality that are of the relevant kind—attempts at humor, social proposals, stories, and so on—but that confuse or fail to animate.

Management: Bores are trying but falling short—they need practice and can learn from your presence and good example. But be careful not to encourage them too much by politely laughing a lot or feigning deep interest. Don't forget your Emily Post: "Alas it is true: 'Be polite to bores and so shall you have bores always round about you.'"*

Self-Promoters

While some killjoys underperform or underwhelm in various ways, other killjoys suck by over-performing. Please shift your attention now to the right-hand branch under "Killjoy (Opt In)" to the category of *self-promoter*.

Remember that social openings are successful when they create copersons. Self-promoters generally have an inflamed self-interest that impedes coperson creation by disrupting the requisite mutual appreciation. They focus all their energy on presenting themselves, leaving little for the appreciation of others. Where killjoys have a tendency to underexpress themselves, self-promoters overexpress themselves. There are different

---

* Emily Post, *Etiquette: In Society, in Business, in Politics, and at Home* (New York: Funk and Wagnalls Company, 1922), 53–54.

ways to over-perform in a social opening, which brings us to the blowhard, the braggart, and the thunder stealer.

Blowhards

The *blowhard* fails to be sensitive to the egalitarian dynamics of the ethics of awesomeness by overrating or misunderstanding the value of his contribution to the social opening. This is a kind of self-absorption that tends to blind him to the fact that, as genuinely interesting or accomplished as he may be, there is limited value in him contributing so much information about his knowledge, interests, life, or achievements.

The blowhard's strategy threatens to be self-undermining in two ways, which are related to the two ways the blowhard can suck. By jumping on every topic and claiming interest or expertise, the blowhard makes it difficult for his copeople to form a coherent image of his individuality beyond the fact that this person is interested in, good at, or knowledgeable about everything. The onslaught of information overwhelms. A second problem arises from the blowhard's manner of delivery. Some blowhards might express interest in and knowledge of every topic in such a way that it seems like all they really care about is talking on and on about these things. And this is not an appreciable feature of individuality.

Management: Don't try to out-blowhard the blowhard. Try to focus the blowhard, who has a tendency to project mastery over every topic. One strategy is to deepen your investigation into whatever topic you're considering and guide the blowhard into novel territory where you are both on the same level. Alternatively, you might invite the blowhard to try a different activity—an unfamiliar game, a new cuisine, a foreign film—so you both have to navigate various uncertainties together. Or just walk away.

If you find yourself with blowhard inclinations, try to remember that pretty much everyone has an expansive individuality. Rein it in a bit and let your actions speak louder than your words. Trust the perceptiveness of your copeople and know that the appreciability of your individuality will emerge over time. Remember too that your worth as a coperson does not depend solely on your accomplishments, interests, knowledge, and so on—give your erudition a rest and let your pure individuality shine now and then.

Braggarts

A slightly suckier but similar type of self-promoter is the *braggart*, who exhibits blowhard characteristics. As we've already established, social openings concern the mutual appreciation of individuality. Braggarts, like blowhards, have managed to understand that in social situations they have to express their individuality, yet they fail to appreciate the symmetrical essence of the arrangement. Unlike blowhards, however, braggarts are focused rather oppressively on themselves. They freely offer themselves up for appreciation, without giving others the opportunity to present themselves. Or, if the opportunity does arise, the braggart tends to lose interest in the conversation and half-asses responses or resorts to thinking in stereotypes. The most extreme braggarts aren't just the most interesting topic of discussion in their own eyes—they're the only genuine topic of discussion.

Management: What makes the braggart suckier than the blowhard is that the latter has more to talk about than herself. As a result, the braggart offers less to get a grip on to steer the social opening in the right direction. The same strategies apply but success might be more difficult.

Thunder Stealers

It's easy to dismiss or have a little fun at the expense of a blowhard or a braggart. They can be fascinatingly out of touch and can really misconstrue the social dynamics. But an especially offensive type of self-promoting suckiness is that of the *thunder stealer*, who tries to undermine the attention that someone else merits and direct it upon himself. The worst thunder stealers cause seismic shifts in attention, reorganizing and even dismantling complex social openings. The thunder stealer is, in a way, a kind of opportunistic braggart, or a self-promoter who exploits other people's expressions for their own gain. They suck like leeches, not only by calling undue attention to themselves but also by exploiting and diminishing the appreciation that other individuals merit.

Management: Thunder stealers can be hard to manage because they strike like lightning and leave the ash of suckiness in their wake. If you can catch the thunder stealer before they act, then you might try redirection. This is another place where direct confrontation or real talk might help. Remind them that it's not their moment.

If you find yourself with thunder-stealing tendencies, don't forget that there is a fine line between being awesome, being game, and being a thunder stealer, depending on the situation. You might think you're being awesome or game when in fact you're shifting social attention in negative ways. So check your gameness. If you think you're being awesome or especially game by bringing five pies to a housewarming party full of the host's specially prepared food, then you might think again. You risk stealing the host's thunder. Better to stick with a tasty beverage or some flowers.

Nonstarters

I would now like to draw your attention to the far right-hand arm of the Suckiness branch. Sticks-in-the-mud and self-promoters have this in common: In one way or another they want to take up the social opening—they opt in but fail to finesse it in the right way. Another type of sucky person lacks even this level of engagement; I call them the *nonstarters*, and they fall into two main categories: the asshole and the fake-ass person. Nonstarters have various ways of blocking the creation of a social opening and so lie outside the ethics of awesomeness. We might think of them as the opposite of awesome, as "social closers," because their habits and modes of engagement tend to rule out social openings from the start. (For this reason, I don't suggest management techniques for these categories because there is no social opening to manage.)

ASSHOLES

Philosopher Aaron James's book *Assholes: A Theory* contains a revealing analysis of the asshole.* He tells us that assholes are people who (mistakenly) feel they are entitled to special advantages in social situations, and they systematically act on this feeling to further their ends and immunize themselves against the legitimate complaints of others. The asshole cuts in line and ignores people who call him out; he drives as if he's the only person on the road and flips you off when you honk at him for being reckless. An asshole would get an invitation to a party and think, "I may or may not go. I'll just decide when it suits me. Obviously the party will be so much better when I show up," with no regard for the host who asks for an RSVP.

Insofar as someone is being an asshole, then, they are placing themselves outside or above the community of individuals, making coperson creation impossible. Hence, assholes are

---

* Aaron James, *Assholes: A Theory* (New York: Doubleday, 2012). See chapter 5, "Asshole Management," for management techniques.

nonstarters. They have difficulty even recognizing social openings because so much of their social engagement comes from a sense of entitlement that in their distorted minds places them above their peers. They socialize not to appreciate and love but to dominate or impress. From the asshole perspective, interactions with them are a privilege for you. The asshole is like the man of "high class" in a socially stratified culture, except he's given himself the high status, and for no good reason.

Some assholes seem to mistakenly think that their money is what entitles them to special privileges in social situations. Recent research suggests that people who regard themselves as wealthy are more likely to cheat, lie, steal, and break the law, even in fictional or pretend situations (for example, when playing Monopoly). One study appears to show that the more expensive your car is, the less likely it is that you will stop for your fellow citizens at a crosswalk (which is the law in California and awesome everywhere).*

FAKE-ASS PEOPLE

When we accept a social opening, we present an aspect of the kind of person we are, and in doing so we give an impression of our individuality. In other words, we issue a persona. *Persona*

---

* See Paul K. Piff, "Wealth and the Inflated Self: Class, Entitlement, and Narcissism," *Personality and Social Psychology Bulletin* 40, no. 1 (2013): 34–43; Paul K. Piff, Daniel M. Stancato, Stéphane Côté, Rodolfo Mendoza-Denton, and Dacher Keltner, "Higher Social Class Predicts Increased Unethical Behavior," *Proceedings of the National Academy of Sciences* 109, no. 11 (2012): 4086–91.

literally means "mask." But this doesn't mean that we are misleading anyone as to who we are or aspire to be. We can wear masks of ourselves, ones that highlight or accentuate our best features—makeup, clothing, tattoos, and our overall style do this.

Fake-ass people wear masks that aren't of themselves. They issue personas that aren't really theirs, or they don't present who they really are or aspire to be. In doing so, they may seem to create or accept social openings—they may seem to express a certain sense of humor, confidence, generosity, and so on. But they're actually nonstarters because they're faking it. Which sucks. Fake-ass people often have ulterior motives. They issue personas not for the sake of real mutual appreciation, but for the sake of convenience, being part of the in-crowd, to gain an upper hand, or to get something they want.

Douchebags

Douchebags are an especially prevalent and troublingly multiplying type of fake-ass person. The douchebag is inseparable from a specific style combined with a certain way of acting and interacting. The douchebag: (1) adopts a mainstream persona, (2) out of an insecurity about and concern for what others think about them, (3) but tries to mask this concern by acting like an asshole, (4) and by doctoring their mainstream persona to seem like an individual.*

---

* *Douchebag* is a heavily male-centric term, but I see no reason why there could not be female douchebags, or douchebagettes.

Consider a mainstream look, like the Frat Jock, Ivy League Preppy, Miami Beach Clubster, L.A. Slickster, or Jersey Shore Bro. Adopting such a look does not make you automatically sucky; there are awesome Jersey Shore Bros and Ivy League Preppies. But the douchebag adopts the look not because it really captures his sense of style but out of a pronounced insecurity—a dominating worry about what people think of him and whether he'll fit in. By adopting the familiar look, he ensures his place in a mainstream community.

That level of insincerity alone is familiar enough. But the douchebag takes it further. His desire to fit in clashes with his desire to stand out. He recognizes that he cannot be too mainstream lest he blend into the crowd of slicksters, preppies, or jocks. He wants to seem privileged or important. So he masks himself even further. He hides his insecure attempt to blend in with a nod to individuality: His pink oxford collar is popped, his eyebrows are manicured, his shirt is very tight and flashy. And he masks his insecurity with a veneer of assholery: You don't want to get in his way or question his motives. If you question his sincerity, he'll question yours; if you threaten his self-appointed place as stronger, better looking, or more entitled, then he'll attack. His jokes are obnoxious, bullyish, and crude; his attachments are thin and fickle. But the douchebag isn't an asshole because he doesn't really have an inflamed self-regard. The douchebag wants to belong. But he also wants to stand out and above, which forces him into fake forms of expression.

Self-Effacers

A very different type of fake-ass person never really allows a clear persona to emerge, in spite of the fact that she seems generally inclined to take up social openings and might even be quite engaged and engaging. This type of fake-ass person obscures or effaces herself, always expressing some character or other, but never making it very clear who she is or what she cares about. She's often making jokes instead of giving straight answers; she hides behind sarcasm and adds an ironic tone to any hint of sincerity. Marcel Proust supplies an example in his character Charles Swann:

> Thus he had grown into the habit of taking refuge in trivial considerations, which enabled him to disregard matters of fundamental importance. Just as he never stopped to ask himself whether he would not have done better by not going into society, but on the other hand knew for certain that if he had accepted an invitation he must put in an appearance, and that afterwards, if he did not actually call, he must at least leave cards upon his hostess, so in his conversation he took care never to express with any warmth a personal opinion about anything, but instead would supply facts and details which were valid enough in themselves and excused him from showing his real capacities. He would be extremely precise about the recipe for a dish, the dates of a painter's birth and death, and the titles of his works. Sometimes, in spite of himself, he

would let himself go so far as to express an opinion on a work of art, or on someone's interpretation of life, but then he would cloak his words in a tone of irony, as though he did not altogether associate himself with what he was saying.[*]

There are several characterizations out there that might capture this person: the ironist or clown. I prefer a more general term—we might use *self-effacer* because this type of person is always erasing any image she paints of herself in the minds of others. Many circa-2002 hipsters—masters of detachment and irony in dress, artistic taste, and styling—were arguably self-effacers.[†]

Tools are a species of self-effacer because they allow themselves to be pawns in other people's games, simply expressing or doing whatever they are expected to by whoever they look up to or whatever group they want to be a part of. It's no wonder that douchebags are often surrounded by a bunch of tools. Another type of tool is the "basic" person who enthusiastically promotes the current trends without really exploring or understanding alternative, less mainstream options. By latching on

---

[*] Marcel Proust, *Swann's Way*, 7 vols., *Remembrance of Things Past* series (New York, NY: Vintage, 1982), p. 229.

[†] As we saw with the construction worker in the previous chapter, and as I discuss further in the next chapter, sometimes being "fake" is an important social strategy. Some people are forced to be fake or to self-efface because of oppressive social conditions. In these cases, it's the social conditions that suck.

to and promoting fads unreflectively they become the perfect marketing tools.

Some people combine self-effacement with other sucky modes. Consider the self-effacing blowhard or braggart, who exhibits blowhard characteristics while noting his excessive contributions and feigning surprise or disbelief. He "cannot believe [he's] talking so much!" and claims that he's "really talking too much about [himself]!" but has no problem continuing and makes no real effort to wrap it up or rein it in.

Modes of Awesomeness

That covers the basic structure of suckiness. It's not the complete and definitive taxonomy—we could continue to fill it in by adding more nodes to the tree, such as *tool* and *micromanager*. You might think about what you would add and where you would place it in the diagram.

Let's shift our attention now to the right side of the diagram under "Awesomeness." There are various ways of not sucking by taking up social openings, and there are a few ways of being awesome by creating social openings. These ways of not sucking and of being awesome are all *modes of awesomeness* in the sense that they are both essential to awesomeness—the state of copersonhood, or the mutual appreciation of individuality. These ways of taking up and creating social openings are the central goods we seek in the ethics of awesomeness, so we will focus our advice and guidance on motivation instead of management.

Down/Taking Up

The general category for not sucking (or non-suckiness) is to be *down*. People who are down take up the social openings presented to them—they receive and respond to your smile or humor; they dance; they appreciate your generosity and spirit. Being down, and therefore not sucking in general, takes a certain ability to imagine what the future holds and to have faith in a potential co-person's ability to actualize that future—we tend to be down when the thought or image of acting on the social opening is enticing.

But there are several ways of being down and not all are equal. As Antanas Mockus notes in the context of teaching, "What people love most is when you write on the blackboard a risky first half of a sentence and then recognize their freedom to write the other half."* People act on that freedom in different ways: being chill, being up, or being game.

Being game, being chill, and being up are ways of responding to awesomeness by taking up the opportunity. That's exactly what Dusty Baker did when Glenn Burke held up his hand for the iconic high five in 1977. When asked whether it was in fact he who invented the high five, Baker said, "No, I

---

* Mockus, "The Art of Changing a City."

didn't invent the high five. All I did was respond to Glenn. That's all I did."* Baker tried to downplay his role, but being down mustn't be downplayed. The ethics of awesomeness is all about taking two (or more) to tango.

CHILL

Some people who are down are flexibly responsive to social openings; they are able and willing to take up a wide range of them. Such people are *chill*. They are mellow navigators of the seas of awesomeness. Remember that many social openings are dynamic: They are composed of shifting activities, changing opportunities, and diverse individuals. Chill people wade through the changing waters—they're down for it all.

Although chill people are very receptive to social openings, they tend not to express much enthusiasm for any particular opening; doing so might conflict with their mellow receptiveness to whatever comes their way. Chill people do have their preferences, but they don't push them to the fore or make a special effort to express them. The reason is that chill people are at least as interested in expressing themselves as they are in engaging with other forms of expressed individuality.

Of course, being chill can be abused, and sometimes people are chill when they shouldn't be. Sometimes we get justifiably

---

* ESPN 30 for 30 Shorts: The High Five. http://www.espn.com/video/clip?id=11253247.

angry, incensed, outraged, or annoyed, and when we express these feelings and someone tells us to "be chill" or "chill out," they might be trying to silence our legitimate voice by appealing to what is otherwise a social virtue. The sense of being chill at issue here is specifically a mode of response to social openings and creative community builders; it's not a way of letting immoral, threatening, or sleazy behavior slide.

Motivation: Chill people have their own cultivated individuality and aren't afraid to express themselves, but they are also especially open to engaging with the expressed preferences of other individuals. In this way, they are the opposite of the sucky preference dictator, who engages social openings only when and to the extent that they align with his preferences and values. The first rule of being chill is keeping an open mind and cultivating sympathetic insight into the interests and values of other individuals. Try to remember the times when being open-minded and flexible led to insight, connection, and joy. Emily Post one more time: "The best ingredients for likeableness are a happy expression of countenance, an unaffected manner, and a sympathetic attitude."[*]

Up

The second way to be down is to be *up*. If you're up for something, then, unlike a chill person, you're merely along for the

---

[*] Post, *Etiquette*.

ride. Chill people have their own values and interests that they are into expressing and satisfying, but they are equally happy to explore and engage with the individualities of others, to play along and be another presence in the name of awesomeness. They are like the dutiful tooth brusher who does the right, clean thing against the call of a warm and cozy bed. The person who is up might feel the pull of a little solo time, of the comforting routine they're used to, but they resist this in the name of awesomeness and take up the social opening. When we are merely up for something we have to do what we can to engage and keep the social opening alive.

Notice the fine line between being up and being a bore. Being a bore is the minimal constraint on being up—you are up exactly to the extent that you avoid being a bore. This can create confusion and lack of clarity between the two. The satirical news publication *The Onion* captures this with its comedic article about "local man Jeff Kirkwood," who:

> . . . was up for absolutely anything except making a definite decision, bar sources reported Friday. "Guys, tonight's going to be epic, and I'm totally game for anything that doesn't require me personally to propose and commit fully to an idea of how to spend the remainder of our night," Kirkwood said, finishing off his first beer and ordering another while affirming that he was "just getting started." . . . "Hell, if you wanted to go bungee jumping right now, I'd be with you all the way

given the fact that everyone else already reached that consensus and were sufficiently enthusiastic that I wouldn't make the final call. So, let's see where the night takes us!"*

The Onion exaggerates the classically up person's willingness to come along and highlights Kirkwood's attempt to stay engaged by feigning enthusiasm. Kirkwood really just wants to come along for the ride—he doesn't want to propose or decide what to do, and reserves his "enthusiasm" for whatever others are enthusiastic about, which is to say he's not *really* enthusiastic about anything. He wants to be up and tries to maintain that position with a nod to spirited interest, but his hollow enthusiasm rings false and threatens to bore.

Motivation: It's good to be up! Even if you can't muster enthusiasm for the social opening, why not play along anyway? Try to recall the two basic reasons we have for taking up social openings: our interest in self-expression, cultivation, and exploration; and the fact that social openings present us with reasons to engage—the activity really is worthwhile, and you really do have something to contribute and gain. We can be up for a social opening even when, for one reason or another, we are not very attuned to these reasons—maybe we're a little tired, burned out, stressed, or distracted. That's when it helps to

* "Area Man Up for Anything Except Being the One Who Makes the Decision," *The Onion*, August 11, 2014: http://www.theonion.com/article/area-man-up-for-anything-except-being-the-one-who--50178.

shift your attention to the other source of reasons to engage: your pure individuality, or your basic ability to break character and explore, express, and play. At the very least, you know that anything can happen and you might be challenged or engaged in unexpected ways. So get up and get down.

GAME

Those who are genuinely enthusiastic about a social opening are *game*. When the thought of acting on a social opening is exciting or enlivening—in the extreme, when it seems that doing so will contribute to our living the kind of life we aspire to live—then we are game. Being game is a matter of being *enthusiastically down*.

One way to get a grip on being game is to consider the rules of improv acting. Improv actors work in groups to improvise a theatrical scene, with often hilarious results. Such actors have to work together on the spot to set up an assortment of characters doing a variety of things. The actors build on the previous actor's contribution to create moments of theatrical fun and comedic brilliance. Improv actor and director David Alger's first rule of improv is essentially to be game. He tells improv actors to say, "Yes! And . . ." When your partner makes a proposal about what the shared activity or event is, Alger's advice is to enthusiastically accept the proposal and build on it in a way that gives other actors an opportunity to say "Yes! And . . ." When one of your partners points right at you and says, "Hey, you big gray cloud! You're going to rain on us!" you should say something like, "Yes, indeed, I really have to pee-pee!"

The difference between being down and being game can be illustrated by considering man's best friend. Most dogs don't suck because they are so game. Dogs were bred not to suck by being bred to be game. Consider the fact that dogs aren't just down for a walk, they are *game* for a walk. They are not chill about it at all. Dogs don't just want to eat, they are *game* to eat; they aren't just down for a ride in the car, they are *game* for a ride in a car.

Going for a ride in a car is better when there's a dog with you who is super into it. People who are game don't just bring hummus and carrots to the party—they get inspired and creative, accepting social openings with communal insight and verve. Their novel contributions animate and inspire others to be game in turn. This is why being game has a special place in the ethics of awesomeness—it's the engine that propels a social opening. Well-expressed enthusiasm tends to spread because it draws attention to the features of the social opening that make it worth taking up. In other words, being game is most effective at getting others to be down, including whoever created the social opening in the first place.

Motivation: Think like a dog. Try to tap into what's best about the social opening and reconnect to the value of your individuality. Recall the times when you propelled a social opening by being game. Think about how much more awesome that social opening was because of you. And don't forget to see yourself as a key player in the context of overall awesomeness.

Awesome/Create

So if you're up, you're down. But if you're down then you aren't necessarily up, or at least not *merely* so, because you might be game—that is, enthusiastically down. Or you might be chill: You might be down for whatever but not especially game and not merely up.

That sums up our discussion of downness. Now we'll shift attention to the second cluster under "Awesomeness." As we established in chapter 2, being *awesome* is a matter of creating opportunities to be down, game, up, and chill. To be awesome is to excel at creating social openings—on the small and large scales—and to therefore be a creator of *copersons* and *crews*.

Rock

Some people combine being awesome with being reliably down in one way or another. Those who are awesome and reliably game *rock*. This makes them very trusty copeople: the friend who loves to take up your social openings and creates her own; the colleague who does everything she can to excel while creating a sense of community by reaching out and helping others however she can; the devoted neighbor whose hospitality and genuineness colors the whole community.

The term *rocks* might not be as popular as it once was—perhaps there are other terms that capture this category. What really matters for our purposes is that we understand the significance of combining being awesome and being game. However, the "rock" metaphor is apt here: People who rock are sturdy purveyors of the ethics of awesomeness, solid as rocks—they are good at creating social openings and excellent at recognizing them and enthusiastically taking them up. But equally apt is the metaphor of a lead singer in a band. Lead singers rock *out* but also often rock in the sense of being awesome. Bands thrive on their audience's reactions, which are in turn reactions to the band's performance and the enthusiasm of the lead singer. The front-person embodies this symbiosis: She sings to the audience, she reacts to their attention, she dances to encourage their appreciation and interest. She's awesome because she and the band are creating the social opening, and she rocks because she's game to absorb the audience's energy and respond in kind. The result is a dynamic sense of community. Such energy is exactly what Jeremy Fry captures when he pretends to rock out—in *pretending* to rock he *actually* rocks.

Motivation: People who rock combine being awesome with being game. So if you're already practiced in being game, try to create more social openings. Or if you're already a social opener, consider the motivation for being game. Another source of motivation can come from envisioning the special kinds of community and connection that people who rock create. They tend to define the character of a crew, community, or culture.

RULE

To rock is to be a kind of leader or keystone in the dynamics of awesomeness. But the metaphor of a leader is present in the ethics of awesomeness in yet another way. Awesome people are good at creating social openings, and people who *rule* are really good at carrying them out in all their glory. They are the master overseers, the benevolent rulers of the social openings they create—the dinner party emcee, the barbecue queen, the road trip realizer.

Ruling comes down to being good at envisioning, organizing, and overseeing extended social openings. This can be difficult because it can easily become self-promoting or preference dictating. For this reason, some people prefer to rule in a chill way, by combining their awesomeness with chillness. They want to create social openings and then let them breathe and live, while watching out, of course, for potential suckiness.

Motivation: When was the last time you tried to create an extended and dynamic social opening? It is one thing to be awesome in everyday life—in the café, workplace, or grocery store—but it's also worth trying to be awesome in more complicated and involved ways. Sometimes we avoid trying because we're so busy or preoccupied, or because the planning can be overwhelming. But it's almost always worth it to plan for awesomeness.

•

Most of us are a curious blend of these types of people. We have our moments of awesomeness and chillness. Sometimes we're game; sometimes we just suck. Healthy crews accommodate this by being dynamic—they shift, grow, and morph, tapping into different sources of energy and forms of self-expression. They also rarely have a single leader, because when they do, they risk turning into structures of suckiness: a fake-ass person dragging everyone down, a braggart surrounded by people being polite, or a self-promoter surrounded by a bunch of tools. It's best for copersons to take turns leading the charge, which is why, even if you're normally a glorious beacon of awesomeness, it's important to practice being down, game, or chill.

This concludes our initial study of the nature and varieties of awesomeness and suckiness. The ethics of awesomeness centers around the model of the creative community builder and, through social openings, the forms of community she gives us the opportunity to take up, cultivate, and create for ourselves. There are many ways of taking up a social opening—being down, up, game, or chill—and there are many ways of opting out (for no good reason): being fake, an asshole, wack, or simply sucky. Finally, there are several ways of opting in, even in good faith, and falling short. The result is an elaborate structure of value, action, and interaction—one that, if the arguments and images of this book are on the right track, is especially important to us.

With our theory in hand, we are in a position to inquire about the broader cultural significance of awesomeness. We can take a step back and think about *why* we value being awesome and not sucking so much these days. Why do we care about awesomeness now? Why are we so upset by suckiness? What are the origins of awesome? And when did we start to care so much?

The answer is complicated and takes us back in time to the 1930s, to the political and cultural struggle for individual self-expression, its effects on American society and culture, and the contemporary desire for a new way of envisioning ourselves and our social lives.

Chapter 5

The Origins of Awesome

WHY IS AWESOMENESS important to us now, in the early twenty-first century? Surely much has been achieved by sucky people, and apparently people engaged in awesomeness are as likely to be acting like Bon Jovi in a music video as they are to be running for office.

There is little doubt that the ideal of awesomeness has stolen our affection. Awesome sings, inspires, and sells. You can include this book among the creative outputs of awesome enthusiasm; it has been, in a way, a kind of love note to awesomeness. But this is a relatively new obsession. It's hard to imagine Jeremy Fry's shenanigans resonating in 1950, and Franklin D. Roosevelt could not have fist-bumped his way into power.

Is this nascent love a good thing? Will it really deliver on what it seems to promise? What exactly *does* awesomeness promise, in the broader scheme of things? Maybe it's just a new toy that we like to play with and not a genuine ideal or a serious way to live our lives.

The New Ideal

If we were to answer in the negative—that awesomeness is not a serious or genuine ideal—then at least from the perspective of the ethics of awesomeness, this book would suck about as much as a book can suck. We would have built up awesomeness only to smack it down. Technically, then, the book would be wack. I suppose that I, as the author of such a wack book, would suck too.

But maybe that's just the cost of philosophical insight. Socrates wasn't always the most pleasant guy to hang with, and you could say far worse about many other philosophers. And after all, being evaluated as sucky isn't the end of the world—as good as it may be, awesomeness isn't the only dimension of value or the only ideal worth having. Our ideals grow, shift, and change; their significance is profound and crystal clear to us in one moment, flat and obscure at best in another.* Ideals shift and

---

* As philosopher Peter Strawson notes, we have many conflicting ideals that come in and out of our lives (ignoring his focus on "men"): "Men make for themselves pictures of ideal forms of life. Such pictures are various and may be in sharp opposition to each other; and one and the same individual may be captivated by different and sharply conflicting pictures at different times. At one time it may seem to him that he should live—even that *a man* should live—in such-and-such a way; at another that the only truly satisfactory form of life is something totally different, incompatible with the first. In this way, his outlook may vary

change not only at the individual level but also at the level of society and culture.

But the fact that ideals are like this is no reason to deny their importance, or to shy away from trying to articulate them, understand their origins, and evaluate their significance, especially when we're in the grip of one as compelling and seemingly urgent as awesomeness. This sense of urgency is something we must take seriously and try to understand clearly.

So why, in the entire history of human life, is this a prominent concern in our time and place? Why value awesomeness? Why would a culture care at all about the communities of individuals that awesomeness institutes?

If the question doesn't grip you, consider the astonishing fact suggested earlier by the story of Glenn Burke: It took our species, *Homo sapiens*, until the 1970s to invent the high five. I find that almost unbelievable. Thousands of years, nearly the entire history of human interaction, of human strife and struggle—a history of hardship and celebration, of love and friendship, of family and community, of serious challenge and soaring triumph—and no high fives. Vigorous handshakes? Of course. Parades? Glorious ones. Pats on the back? Time and again. Hugs and kisses? So many! But no high fives. Why?

To answer this question, and to understand the origins and cultural significance of awesome, we have to go back to the

radically, not only at different periods of his life, but from day to day, even from one hour to the next." ("Social Morality and Individual Ideal," *Philosophy* 36, no. 136 [1961]: 1–17.)

1930s, to the beginnings of a momentous struggle for individual self-expression—one that opened a space for awesomeness to emerge.

Be Cool (or Not)

In the 1930s, the pursuit of individual self-expression began to have a shaping influence on American society and culture. We see this most clearly with the emergence and influence of "cool" as a powerful personal style—a new way of cultivating and expressing one's individuality, and of emphasizing in appearance and demeanor the importance of doing so.

As many of us think of coolness, the quintessentially "cool" person maintains a comfortable distance, always around but never fully present or committed. He's committed instead to maintaining an air of social skepticism or projecting a sense that he sees through and stands above it all. Think of Marlon Brando in *The Wild One* (1953), or Steve McQueen. Better yet, think of James Dean in *Rebel Without a Cause* (1955), in which he plays Jim Stark, the rebel, the disaffected youth, the jobless teen in work boots. The rebel Stark has no real reason to be cool, to project an alluring air of skepticism and distance. As one film poster states, he is "the bad boy from a good family." He is a rebel *without a cause*, a bored suburbanite rebelling for the sake of rebelling. Brando, playing Johnny Strabler in *The Wild One*, famously suggests he's attracted to the same kind of cause-free coolness. He is asked, "Hey Johnny, what are you rebelling against?" His reply: "Whaddaya got?"*

If these men really have no cause, then they have no reason to act like they're above or outside it all—"James Dean cool," as we might call it, can suck. The James Dean cool person might be—or *seem* to be—down, but they risk being half-assers, self-promoters, or even thunder stealers; they might come to the party, so to speak, but they stay at a cool distance from it, only half-committing, projecting an air of superiority or the promise of something better—and for no real reason at all.

It's interesting that the people we associate with James Dean cool are often white men: We might also include Humphrey Bogart, Jack Kerouac, and Frank Sinatra. Some women might seem to resonate with something like James Dean cool—Janis Joplin (especially in the early 1960s), Edie Sedgwick, and Billie Holiday—but it would be misleading. There's a good reason for this: You can't be a rebel without a cause unless you're really without cause, and if you were anything other than a straight white man in the 1950s—if you were black, or a woman, or gay, or trans—then you had many a reason to rebel.

Of course, white men did have causes that a social affectation of distance and allure could address. Coolness could express resilience in the face of pressure to conform to an increasingly

---

* There's almost no end to the books and essays on cool, starting almost as soon as coolness emerged and continuing to this day. See Norman Mailer's 1957 essay "The White Negro."

bland culture that compelled everyone to fit the mainstream corporate mold.* A pressure so acute, Norman Mailer thought, that "One could hardly maintain the courage to be individual, to speak with one's own voice."† When he is asked, "Hey Johnny, what are you rebelling against?" Strabler might have replied: "Well, frankly, I'm rebelling against the idea that my individual and creative thinking is inferior to conformist, business-friendly, collective decision making. That's why I make an effort to resist, to not conform, even in like-minded and generally affable social situations. Cheers!"

What it means to be cool has evolved over the decades. Another meaning, prominent in the 1980s and still with us today, applies to people who are aware of what is mainstream and popular and resist it by engaging with culture that is less easily digestible, more challenging, or more socially and politically aware. Cool people and cool things in this sense don't fit into mainstream culture and don't even try. Uncool people, in contrast, are either blithely unaware of what is or isn't mainstream—they aren't in the know—or they are enthusiastic mainstream ("basic") cultural agents. Cool people in this context are rebels with an anticorporate or at least anti-mainstream cause.

This anti-mainstream sense of *cool* is still with us, but these days the term can even mean the exact opposite. The "cool"

---

* A classic account of this is William H. Whyte's *The Organization Man* (New York: Simon & Schuster, 1956).
† Mailer, "The White Negro."

thing is the current fad, the collectively recognized fun thing to do—the thing to selfie with or Instagram.* William Finnegan captures this in his Pulitzer Prize–winning memoir, *Barbarian Days: A Surfing Life*, when he writes about how cool surfing has become: "Surfers hope bleakly that surfing will one day become, like rollerblading, uncool. Then, perhaps, millions of kooks [inexperienced surfers] will quit and leave the waves to the die-hards. But the corporations selling the idea of surfing are determined, of course, to 'grow the sport.' Some underground panache may be useful for marketing, but really, the more mainstream the merrier."†

The fact that *cool* can simultaneously mean one thing and its very opposite suggests that we have lost our hold on its significance.‡ So what exactly did we lose our grip on? Where did *cool* come from, anyway? And why did we care about it so much that it became deeply embedded in and ultimately distorted by our social and economic culture?

A look at its origins shows that *cool* is more complicated than even this—and far more awesome. The true descendant of the original *cool* is neither James Dean cool, anti-mainstream cool, nor mainstream cool. *Awesome* is its rightful heir.

---

* Malcolm Gladwell writes about this sense of *cool* in his 1997 *New Yorker* essay "The Coolhunt."

† Penguin Books (2016), 419.

‡ For an account of how *cool* found a secure place in the business and marketing world, see Thomas Frank's *The Conquest of Cool: Business Culture, Counterculture, and the Rise of Hip Consumerism* (Chicago: University of Chicago Press, 1998).

Lester Young

Cool began as a rebellion with a very serious cause. Lester "Prez" Young, the revered and exceptionally original American jazz saxophonist of the mid-twentieth century, is the true inventor of cool.* He performed in a racist era, when whites imposed racist norms on black performers—actors, comedians, musicians, and others. They were expected to always smile on stage, entertain, and generally be jovial and accepting of whatever their white audience wanted. In addition to their immoral oppression, whites were essentially forcing black performers into fake-assery, and the performers were getting fed up with it.

Lester Young resisted this Uncle Tom culture in part by adopting a detached and mellow style and signaling his intention to not observe the "rules." Onstage he played tilting his saxophone sideways, soloing at a nearly 45-degree angle, turned away from the audience. He often wore sunglasses while performing, so that the audience couldn't discern his facial expression. His cool stage presence effectively shifted the focus of the performance from the Uncle Tom goal of pleasing the audience to the music-centered goal of playing excellent original jazz and directing the audience to pay sympathetic attention.

---

* Joel Dinerstein makes this case in his excellent essay "Lester Young and the Birth of Cool," in *Signifyin(g), Sanctifyin', & Slam Dunking: A Reader in African American Expressive Culture*, ed. Gena Dagel Caponi (Amherst: University of Massachusetts Press, 1999), 239–76; see also Dinerstein's book *The Origins of Cool in Postwar America* (Chicago: University of Chicago Press, 2017).

Young's coolness extended beyond the stage to become an all-encompassing personal style, as original as it was alluring. He adopted an almost indecipherable slang, including the word *cool*, that made his speech as difficult to understand as it was mysteriously attractive. As cultural historian and Tulane University English professor Joel Dinerstein writes, "Young's whole life was self-consciously dedicated to being original—in his music, in his mannerisms, in his style of detachment—as if being original was the vital force of human life itself."* His individual self-expression was so original and appealing that other people—actors, suburban youth, people without a cause, and even many jazz musicians—could not help but adopt it for themselves.†

Lester Young's cool style can be understood only in the context of his ideal of a better social and artistic culture. He cultivated a stylistic strategy to counter racist, immoral, and sucky norms that affected his artistic community. This was a strategy meant to generate interpersonal norms that would bolster that community's ability to express itself personally and artistically and be appreciated for the individuals they were. Once we appreciate this feature of Young's cool style, we can appreciate its connection to awesomeness. His style was very different from a

---

* Dinerstein, "Lester Young and the Birth of Cool."
† Some readers will recall seeing a young Bill Clinton running for president and trying to appeal to the American people by overtly adopting Lester Young's style, playing saxophone in sunglasses on *The Arsenio Hall Show* to wild cheers of "woot woot woot!" from an enthusiastic audience.

social affectation of distance and allure adopted for its own sake by suburban youth and movie stars. Young's cool was creative community building of the most stylish and awesome order.

The awesomeness of Lester Young's cool is not only reflected in his personal style. It also shines through his artistic style, in what jazz legend Dizzy Gillespie called his "cool, flowing style" of playing the saxophone. The subdued, cool texture drew the listener into Young's melodic universe. As B. B. King notes: "Prez invented cool. Rather than state a melody, he suggested it. He barely breathed into his horn, creating an intimacy that gave me chills."[*] Young's coolness, reflected in his musical style, created an awesome intimacy—a kind of inviting, musical social opening. His whole style, then, both as a person *and* as an artist, was awesome.[†]

Young's awesome coolness was cultivated and flourished in the context of Count Basie's band—an especially fertile context for awesomeness. As Joel Dinerstein writes, "The implicit challenge of playing in Basie's band was to maintain one's *individuality* in the face of a powerful *collective* rhythmic drive. Here then is the first contribution of big-band swing to African American cool: a cultural form that publicly displayed *the fight for individual self-expression within a larger unit*."[‡]

---

[*] B. B. King and David Ritz, *Blues All Around Me: The Autobiography of B.B. King* (New York, NY: Avon Books, 1996), p. 105.

[†] Young's life also demonstrates our earlier point that a person can be awesome without being extroverted. He was often described as aloof, alien, shy, and elusive.

[‡] Dinerstein, "Lester Young and the Birth of Cool," 251, emphasis added.

The interpersonal dynamics of a big band—indeed, of many bands—incorporate a significant tension between individuality and community. You have to be yourself and play your instrument, but you also have to integrate into the larger whole. If you're too much of an individual, then you ruin the music—your solos don't mesh; your rhythm is off. But if you're too willing to blend in, then you fade away—your solos don't inspire; your rhythm doesn't rev the engine and drive things forward. But when everyone in the band is doing this well—when each member is being an individual in and for a community—the tension is resolved into something beautiful: the musical, communal expression of the mutual appreciation of individuality.

This is the beauty that Lester Young's cool cultivated and that awesomeness promises.

Individuality and Community: A Tension

It is no coincidence that the high five emerged shortly after American society, with the hard work, daring, and genius of people like Lester Young, E. D. Nixon, Rosa Parks, Dr. Martin Luther King Jr., Gloria Steinem, Frank Kameny, and many others, began a seismic shift in American culture—a shift we have yet to fully process and socially realize.

In the mid- to late twentieth century there was a dramatic upheaval of laws, codes of formality, and social norms and roles that radically changed and continue to change the way we interact. The civil rights movement, women's liberation, the sexual revolution, LGBT progress, and radical changes in artistic culture, among other things, dramatically altered our lives from the ground up—from how we publicly behave and interact to who we can aspire to be and be with.

Many of those laws and norms were morally atrocious. Racist, repressive, sexist, homophobic—they were (and are) oppressive and unjust, and there was a profound moral imperative to change them. But there was another important factor motivating this cultural revolution: Those social norms, exclusionary laws, and codes of formality severely restricted the forms of individuality and expression available even to those who benefited from them the most (middle- to upper-class straight cis white men). The desire to fully and freely develop and express our individuality began to inform our culture at the deepest levels.

We see this in the emergence of the awesome coolness developed and cultivated by black musicians who fought against sucky fake-assery and for the free expression of individual style. But they weren't the only people who rightly felt that mainstream American culture smothered their humanity by denying them freedom of individual expression. We can't forget women who couldn't follow their wildest—or even basic—dreams, who were expected to stay at home cleaning, cooking, and child-rearing; gay men and women who couldn't pursue their romantic desires, who were forced to hide in the shadows; all who felt oppressed by society's expectation that they marry early and remain monogamous, who couldn't freely express and explore their sexuality; people everywhere who shuddered at the thought of mainstream American life—high school, college, marriage, career, suburban house, children, and so on—and who dreamed of something else, who were pressured to stifle those dreams and toe the line; people who, more generally, could not accept the forms of authority, the rigid expectations, the circumscribed and monolithic communities . . . unfortunately, I could easily go on. These people yearned, with justice on their side and awesomeness in view, for a more open, creative, accepting, and appreciative culture.

With the cultural and political revolutions of the 1960s, the desire to fully express ourselves and develop our individuality in all its glory started to have a shaping influence on society. Although we are still deep in the process of making it happen,* the complete downfall of oppressive norms, codes, and forms of community would mean that society is open to people being gay or straight, man or woman, religious or atheist—we could be rockers, entrepreneurs, rappers, preachers, punks, hippies, philosophers, skaters, or some strange or exciting combination of these. We could try to be anything our individual ideals could dream up. We could act like Bon Jovi at halftime and get a crew of strangers to play around with us; we could rectify the

---

* For example, five states still have no laws against hate crimes: Arkansas, Indiana, South Carolina, Wyoming, and Georgia, whose hate crime statute was struck down by the Georgia Supreme Court as recently as 2004.

awesomeness of public space through art, or don a superhero costume in daily life.

But those social norms, laws, traditions of community, and codes of formality established a range of connections and forms of culture that glued large swaths of society together and satisfied our profound need for community, at least for those privileged enough to be included. The fight for individual expression, along with other economic and political changes, weakened long-standing bonds of community. Beginning in the 1960s, neighborhood and family ties loosened, local associations disbanded, church attendance declined, political participation waned, and ties of social and economic class weakened.* These ties were difficult to repair in the following years, as steady work became harder to find when corporations became more powerful and spread themselves across the United States and the globe. Increased travel, more short-term work, and a widening gap between rich and poor put further strains on American social ties.

The result of these cultural, economic, and political shifts is a progressively relaxed, dynamic, open, and accommodating social and civic environment. But it's an environment that obscures

---

* Robert D. Putnam, political scientist and Malkin Professor of Public Policy at the Harvard University John F. Kennedy School of Government, documents this extensively and argues at length and with considerable empirical evidence that "social capital"—our networks of personal bonds and community ties—has sharply declined (roughly) since the 1960s. See *Bowling Alone: The Collapse and Revival of American Community* (New York: Simon & Schuster, 2000) and, with Lewis Feldstein and Don Cohen, *Better Together: Restoring the American Community* (New York: Simon & Schuster, 2003).

and even destroys many of the underlying commonalities, traditions, and compatible lives and values that, when expressed and appreciated, satisfied our need for community. And although many of those old forms of community needed to be replaced with something fair, just, and engaging, we are still struggling to find the right way to do that.

This tension between individuality and community cuts to the heart of a more general difficulty faced by any conception of a society worth hoping for. We love exploring and cultivating our individuality and expressing ourselves. We want to distinguish ourselves, explore, develop, and display our values and talents, flaunt our style; we want to create and cultivate our own sense of a life worth living and express ourselves in the process of living that life. We aren't built to strictly follow predetermined social roles, do whatever someone else tells us we should do, float our lives down the mainstream, or always bend to the general will. We want to explore, cultivate, and express our individuality.

But at the same time we want to feel that we are part of a *community* of people. We want to connect with others, be appreciated for who we are, and feel at home in our appreciation of others. Our desire to cultivate and express ourselves is at least as important as our desire to be part of a community—to cultivate that sense of social joy, that intimacy and rapport we feel when we connect and appreciate.

In short, we want to love ourselves *and* our neighbors; we want to stand out but stand *together.*

These two desires are fundamental in our lives, but they naturally conflict. Social and political theorist Emma Goldman appreciated this problem as early as 1911: "The problem that confronts us today, and which the nearest future is to solve, is how to be one's self and yet in oneness with others, to feel deeply with all human beings and still retain one's own characteristic qualities."*

It is important to appreciate this problem in depth and detail, and we can do so by using the resources we developed in the previous chapter. If you're too eager to be an individual, too focused on standing out and expressing yourself, then you risk being unintelligible to, or alienated from, the wider culture—you risk coming off as a vile self-promoter, "cool" thunder stealer, fake-ass person, wack, or simply sucky. And if you're too eager to belong, too deferential to the wider community, too willing to adopt its values and go with the mainstream flow, then you risk being overlooked or uninteresting—you risk coming off as basic, douchey, toolish, or a bore.

Notice that this conflict or tension is not the more familiar one between our free pursuit of individual expression and our

* See her essay "The Tragedy of Women's Emancipation," in *Anarchism and Other Essays,* ed. Will Jonson, 2nd rev. ed. (New York and London: Mother Earth Publishing Association, 1910), 219–31.

responsibility to our community. We know we can't just do whatever we want—*We live in a society!*—and we must take into everyday account the fact that we are one among many. Nor does it concern the issue of whether the individual or the community is the more fundamental unit of political significance. Rather, this is a tension or conflict within our conception of freedom, within our sense of what a good life is in a free society. It is a real struggle to strike a balance between cultivating our individuality and being part of a community—a struggle that we can easily lose, ending up disaffected, bored, or hopeless.

Or worse. Various distortions of self and community can be diagnosed as resulting from this tension, from relatively mild douchebaggery to hate groups, cults, and narcissism. Hate groups create a wack individuality and perverse sense of belonging by collectively mutilating their ability to appreciate individuals. Cult members and religious fanatics find community through *group* individuality, but at the cost of their own personal individuality (and, arguably, real community). Narcissists and certain eccentrics alienate themselves from any desire for community by inflating the importance of their individuality. We recognize these groups and individuals as aberrations because they don't sit well in a flourishing free society, in part because they fail to really resolve the tension between the pursuit of individuality and the pursuit community that informs an important conception of a meaningful life.

And, it is crucial to note, this tension exists at the larger level of social and political organization. A society that promotes too much individuality is at risk of lacking a substantial and satisfying sense of community, while one that promotes too much commonality or conformity risks being a community of bores, killjoys, or fake-ass people. Or worse. Fascists deal with the tension by eschewing individualism and, through a blend of violence, false charm, propaganda, and coercion, forcing everyone to share the state-approved values and attitudes.

A good society must find a way to resolve this tension, while respecting the legitimacy of both values and not excluding or diminishing people because of their race, sex, abilities, gender, or sexual preferences—that is, not excluding or diminishing individuals in pursuit of individuality. This truth at the level of social organization also holds at the level of individual aspiration: We must cultivate our individuality in a way that complements our sense of community and vice versa.

Individuality and Community: A Resolution

What if a value we all loved, an ideal we all shared—one that brought us together in pursuit of a society-shaping blend of individuality and community—were awesomeness?

Awesome people combine the rebel spirit with the quest for community. The sense of "community" here is, again, that of a community of individuals, or people who appreciate one another *as* individuals—either as concrete individuals with cultivated values and tastes or as pure individuals in their capacity to play, explore, and express. Awesome people are excellent at finding creative ways to institute this kind of community, not by convincing us to share the same values—we don't all have to be mainstream, Christian, straight, or highly educated; we don't even have to have worked out what our concrete values are—but by encouraging us to express ourselves and appreciate one another through creative community building.

A promising hypothesis, then, is that we see in awesomeness a new sense of style, a new and necessary way of thinking about ourselves and what matters to us—one that seeks to reconcile our desires for community and individuality by redrawing what it means to have a community and be an individual. Restricting community to the sharing of mainstream values doesn't work for a free and diverse society, and our individuality is not something we find sitting there when we introspect—it's something we need to explore, cultivate, refine, and express with others. We need a new ideal or plan for thinking about ourselves, and being awesome is this plan.

Our love of awesomeness emerged from our collective exploration and slow discovery of ways of bringing community and connection back into our increasingly self-expressive, individualistic culture. We identify with awesomeness because it promises to reconcile these values in a way that actually promotes a kind of individualism without threatening—indeed while creating—community. Awesomeness envisions no conflict between individuality and community; it promises to institute a long-sought sociocultural arrangement in which the cost of community is not the loss of individuality, and our pursuit of individuality is not only compatible with but also essential to a new kind of community.

Awesome Style

Style and awesomeness go hand in hand. That might not be very surprising given our discussion so far, but there's also a simple argument for it: Roughly, style is the art of expressing your individuality. Awesomeness requires the mutual appreciation of individuality. And if your individuality is to be appreciated, then it must be expressed. Therefore, style is essential to awesomeness.

But awesome style requires care, lest we be wack, basic, self-promoters, or simply sucky. To understand what *awesome style* is, we first need to know what style is.

Simple philosophical reflection on style reveals it to be confusing. A person's style, we often think, is his way of doing things—the way he dresses, talks, sits, and walks. But at the same time we tend to think that not everyone has style—that having style is rare, or at least challenging; it is something we have to work at to achieve. But notice that if style is just your way of doing things, then everyone has some style or other because everyone has a way of doing things. So why do we also think that only some people have style, that it's something to work at and achieve? Either only some people have style or everyone has style—we can't have it both ways.

There is also some confusion about how we value or admire style. On the one hand, we tend to think that pursuing style is trivial or frivolous—that there are far better things to do with our time and energy. When Mark Zuckerberg was asked about his apparent lack of style, why he simply wears the same gray shirt and jeans nearly every day, he echoed this opinion: "I feel like I'm not doing my job if I spend any of my energy on things that are silly or frivolous about my life."[*] On the other hand, though, we admire people who we think have style. They can dazzle us, amaze us, and send us into a frenzy of inspiration. People with style—Lester Young, Sara and Gerald Murphy, Josephine Baker, Yves Saint Laurent, David Bowie, Patti Smith, Beyoncé, Cate Blanchett, Michelle Obama, and many others—can even help form our personal ideals, giving our lives meaning and direction. So is style trivial and unimportant or is it dazzling, meaningful, and important? It is either trivial and unimportant or admirable and meaningful—we can't have it both ways.

Some philosophers and art historians have tried to understand style as the expression of personality.[†] But this doesn't help our

---

[*] Eugene Kim, "Here's the Real Reason Mark Zuckerberg Wears the Same T-Shirt Every Day," *Business Insider UK*, November 7, 2014, http://uk.businessinsider.com/mark-zuckerberg -same-t-shirt-2014-11?r=US&IR=T.

[†] An influential philosophical statement of this view is Jenefer M. Robinson's essay "Style and Personality in the Literary Work," *Philosophical Review* 94, no. 2 (1985): 227–47.

confusion. We all have a personality and we all effortlessly—indeed inescapably and unreflectively—express our personalities in nearly everything we do. If style is the expression of personality, then it would seem to be easy and of little interest. So what is so great about style when it captivates, inspires, and enthralls?

It's more illuminating to think of style as the expression of our *personal ideals*—not simply the personality each person has but the individual he or she aspires to be.* Our ideals articulate our admirable qualities and aspirations, so this view sees style as bound up with imagination. This helps us understand why we think style is an achievement—it's not easy to really embody our ideals; it's something we must work at and strive for. It also helps us make sense of why we might idealize people who have achieved great style. People whose style we admire are beautifully expressing ideals that we ourselves might identify with and aspire to.

Now that we have a better understanding of style, what is it to have *awesome* style?

•

Let us hark back, if we can, to some of the first intimations of awesomeness in the writings of the great early theorist of modern life: Charles Baudelaire (1821–1867), the infamous French

---

* I argue for this view in my paper "Personal Style and Artistic Style," in *Philosophical Quarterly* 65, no. 261 (2015): 711–31.

poet, translator (of Edgar Allan Poe), and critic of art, fashion, and culture. Baudelaire was born just as a new era in Western culture was emerging. Kings and queens were losing power, along with the social order their reigns had instituted. The industrial revolution had just transformed Europe socially and economically, and a historic series of democratic milestones was sweeping the west. He saw the aftermath of the founding of the United States of America and the first French Revolution, he lived during the 1848 French Revolution and the passing of the United Kingdom's Slavery Abolition Act, and he witnessed the rise of democracy in Denmark and the Netherlands. As people flooded into cities in search of work, a new working class ballooned along with an increasingly diverse middle class. A new modern era was born—one that was less regal, authoritarian, and rigid and far more democratic and individualistic. Baudelaire was living in and writing about Paris as it anchored this change.*

Baudelaire thought there was a certain potential for beauty in this new life, a new beauty that one could create for oneself and find reflected in people's dress and demeanor: "The idea of beauty which man creates for himself imprints itself on his whole attire, crumples or stiffens his dress, rounds off or squares his gesture, and in the long run even ends by subtly penetrating

---

* It was nowhere near a pretty picture, though, as working conditions were horrifying and a giant gap between rich and poor kept the working class overworked and disempowered (among other terrible things).

the very features of his face. Man ends by looking like his ideal self."*

In other words, there is a certain *style* of the modern individual—one that expresses the new era's special sense of beauty. Baudelaire sought to uncover this sense of beauty; he sought "to discover whether we possess a specific beauty, intrinsic to our new emotions."†

What exactly is that style, that specific beauty? Baudelaire praised Constantin Guys, a Dutch-born war reporter, watercolor painter, and illustrator who Baudelaire thought captured this style perfectly. Guys found a special beauty and joy in the fractured hustle of modern life. He felt connected to the public—and to life in public—and he expressed this sense of beauty in his paintings and illustrations as well as in his everyday life.

Guys had a special capacity for curiosity among and joy in diverse people. He saw the throngs of public life with creative and childlike eyes—as a beautiful expression of humanity that electrifies. He thought poorly of anyone who was simply bored by others: ". . . any man who is not weighed down with a sorrow so searching as to touch all his faculties, and who is bored in the heart of the multitude, is a fool! a fool! and I despise him!"‡

---

* See his essay "The Painter of Modern Life," in *Selected Writings on Art and Literature* (New York: Penguin, 1992), p. 400, translation slightly altered.
† Ibid.
‡ Ibid.

In other (less French) words, such a person sucks. Guys hated "blasé" people, like those dandies who share with him "a quintessence of character and a subtle understanding of all the moral mechanisms of this world" but who mask it behind an aspiration to "cold detachment"* (or sucky coolness).

Guys, in contrast, is a "lover of life," a kind of "man child" with a "childlike perceptiveness"—he is "a genius for which no aspect of life has become *stale*."† This childlike genius approaches the crowd of humanity with creative eyes: "The lover of life makes the whole world his family. . . . Thus the lover of universal life enters into the crowd as though it were an immense reservoir of electrical energy. Or we might liken him to a mirror as vast as the crowd itself; or to a kaleidoscope gifted with consciousness, responding to each one of its movements and reproducing the multiplicity of life and the flickering face of all the elements of life. He is an 'I' with an insatiable appetite for the 'non-I.'"‡

In other (less French) words, he is an individual who has a creative hunger for the community of individuals. In expressing this hunger in his art and his own life, he becomes an individual, an "I," whose defining ideal is to engage others with a joyful and creative spirit. In still other (less French) words: His style is awesome.

---

* Ibid.
† Ibid.
‡ Ibid.

Awesome style, then, is style that projects an "I" with a yearning for the "non-I." Or, to adopt a phrase from philosopher John Dewey, it is style through which we cultivate our own gardens, but without a fence—gardens that are inseparable from the world, open to others, that attract and invite others to engage and appreciate.* Awesome style embodies the ability to cultivate individuality within a "collective rhythmic drive"—within, indeed *for*, the life and culture of individuals in pursuit of individuality. It is style whose central ideal is awesomeness, style that expresses the ideal of being awesome, or style keyed for community.

•

Of course, it took more time and much more political and cultural change for people with awesome style to really capture our collective imagination. Our hypothesis is that our love of awesomeness is a love for a style that promises a culturally important twist on and blend of individuality and community—a style that did not begin to flourish until (roughly) after the cultural revolutions of the 1960s, when our legitimate demand for individual expression merged and clashed with our deep desire for community.

---

* "To gain an integrated individuality, each of us needs to cultivate his own garden. But there is no fence about this garden: it is no sharply marked-off enclosure. Our garden is the world, in the angle at which it touches our own manner of being." (John Dewey, *Individualism Old and New* (New York: Prometheus Books 1999), 82–83.

If this hypothesis is on the right track, then we should be able to find forms of culture that emerged or flourished after the 1960s and that, in one way or another, embody the ethics of awesomeness. We should be able to locate not only individual awesome actions—which of course we have done—but larger cultural forms and movements that embody or reflect this new ethos.

Chapter 6

Awesome Culture

THE CONCEPT OF "culture" is vague and confusing. It seems to include everything from what we eat and how we talk to how we build cities and structure government. It was *The Merriam-Webster Dictionary*'s "word of the year" in 2014 because it saw the biggest jump in searches that year. And to add to the muddle, we have pop culture, celebrity culture, consumer culture, car culture, start-up culture, and hookup culture, among many other "cultures" that occupy our attention.

In its broadest sense, *culture* refers to the customs, attitudes, and ways of life of a group of people. We might be interested in various "cultures" in this sense because they are novel, exciting, sordid, or just so different from our own. But a more specific sense of the word concerns the ways we spend our time—the activities we pursue and things we create—when we aren't too hungry, oppressed, jobless, and stressed, or weakened by violence or war. Culture in this sense interests us because it is what we seek when we have the time and peace of mind to cultivate our individuality, explore the city, wander into the museum, volunteer at the clinic or shelter, pick up a book, meet up with a friend, or buy a ticket to the basketball game.

In this second sense, culture is something we seek and create to occupy our "free" time in pursuit of personal and social enrichment. Through culture in this context we amplify our individual and collective quality of life. This is the proper domain of awesomeness, the place where the ethics of awesomeness can fully take hold and really thrive. To appreciate the broader cultural currents of emerging awesomeness, we will have to look at how people use their free time and extra resources to create and engage in such life-enhancing pursuits.

Our case will be strongest if we focus on how the ethos of awesome is affecting *central* or *paradigmatic* kinds of cultural activity. To this end, we will look at forms of altruism (how we use our free time and resources to help others), athleticism (how we use our time for fun and recreation), civic life (how we freely engage and interact in public space), and art (how we create and appreciate it).

Awesome culture is primarily a culture of social creativity in action, in which the creative sociality centrally involves the cultivation, exploration, and appreciation of individuality. Such activity embodies the ethics of awesomeness by emphasizing creative community building, the cultivation of awesome style, and the mutual appreciation of individuality.

Altruism

Yale University's endowment is well over $20 billion; Harvard University's is $36 billion (with $43 billion in total wealth). To put that in perspective, the combined wealth of these small private universities rivals the GDP of the Dominican Republic, and each far outweighs the $4 billion endowment of the public University of California, Berkeley, which enrolls nearly ten thousand more students than Harvard and Yale combined. If there are any universities in the history of the universe that have needed money least, it's these two.

Yet in 2013, Yale received its largest gift ever—$250 million from Charles B. Johnson, the businessman and enthusiastic Republican donor. Two years later, Harvard topped that when its School of Engineering and Applied Sciences received a $400 million gift from hedge fund manager John A. Paulson, who made $15 billion using credit default swaps to bet against the US subprime mortgage lending market. Following the donation, the engineering school was renamed the Harvard

John A. Paulson School of Engineering and Applied Sciences. Paulson also received a tax break of nearly $200 million.*

Such charity might inspire a certain flavor of amazement, but it is hardly awesome, especially when compared with, to take an obvious example, the Awesome Foundation—"a global community advancing the interest of awesome in the universe, $1,000 at a time."† Members of the Awesome Foundation are self-described "guerrilla philanthropists" who give out no-strings-attached microgrants to artists, innovators, activists, organizers—anyone who wants to do something awesome. Each chapter consists of a board of trustees who donate a hundred dollars of their own money each month. The trustees survey various proposals and give as many grants as they can to the most awesome projects.

So what do they mean by "awesome"? Their take on awesomeness is strikingly similar to the theory developed here: "Awesome projects . . . tend to challenge and expand our understanding of our individual and communal potentials. They bring communities together, casting aside social inhibitions and boundaries for a moment. They spark an instant of joy and delight and inspire a long-term hope for a more Awesome future."‡

The first Awesome Foundation project, funded in Boston in

---

* Kellie Woodhouse, "Does Harvard Need Your Money?" *Inside Higher Ed*, June 5, 2015, https://www.insidehighered.com/news/2015/06/05/400-million-gift-harvard-sets-debate-about-philanthropy-wealthy-institutions.
† http://www.awesomefoundation.org/.
‡ "FAQ," Awesome Food, http://www.awesomefood.net/faq/.

2009, involved making a gigantic multicolored hammock for everyone to enjoy in a public park. As of 2015, dozens of autonomous Awesome Foundation chapters have sprung up around the world, including ones in Paris, Nairobi, Moscow, Yerevan, Dubai, Lusaka, and all over the United States and Canada. And they fund a range of projects, including converting old buses into showers for the homeless, making widely distributable fuel from wood-charcoal waste, creating community murals, and designing "pop-up experiences" like the reenactment of the famous boulder escape scene from the Indiana Jones film *Raiders of the Lost Ark* in downtown Washington, DC.

While acknowledging that both forms of giving deliver benefits and embody values, it is important to be clear about their differences. The first is an ostentatious display that benefits a group that is least in need of benefit and shows off the wealth of the donor. It is arguably a self-promoting display of individual excellence, which is to say it sucks. However, that's not to say that it is entirely bad. It doesn't take deep insight to see that there are *some* good things about giving lots and lots of money to people who already have lots and lots of money—for one thing, they get lots and lots of money. But as a self-promoting display it also sucks.

The second form of giving shows us how to be altruistically awesome. It is modest and innovative, and focuses on creative community-building efforts. It might not be the all-things-considered absolute best way to use money for good—if such can be reasonably determined—but the world is decidedly more awesome with giant colorful public hammocks, community murals, and pop-up fun.

A more focused effort in awesome giving is Ron Finley's guerrilla gardening, which began in 2010. Finley was overwhelmed by the health problems he observed in his community in South Central Los Angeles. He noticed that he had far better access to fast food than to decent produce, and this was taking a toll on the health of South Central residents. When he noticed all the neglected city land in the neighborhood, he decided to "get gangsta" with his shovel. He planted seeds in an unused strip of land near his home and grew a vibrant community garden, giving neighbors access to fresh and healthy fruits, vegetables, and seeds—sunflowers, kale, pomegranates—and the opportunity to explore a wider variety of food options. His efforts, along with similar projects in other states and countries, have inspired others to literally grow a better, healthier community by transforming neglected land into fresh, free produce.

Finley thinks of this effort in terms of art:

I'm an artist. Gardening is my graffiti. I grow my art. Just like a graffiti artist—where they beautify walls. Me: I beautify lines, parkways; I use the garden, the soil, like it's a piece of cloth. And the plants and the trees—that's my embellishment for that cloth. You'd be surprised what the soil can do if you let it be your canvas; you just couldn't imagine how amazing a

sunflower is and how it affects people. So what happened? I
have witnessed my garden become a tool for the education, a
tool for the transformation of my neighborhood. To change
the community, you have to change the composition of the
soil. We are the soil.*

Finley's community-building altruism invites his neighbors to
be up, game, and chill—awesome qualities that the city's Bu-
reau of Street Services severely lacked when they gave him a
citation and told him to remove his "overgrown vegetation" or
pay four hundred dollars. Finley refused and a warrant was issued for his arrest.

My first thought was: *Bring it*. It's a stupid, antiquated law
that needs to be changed. There was no healthy food in the
neighborhood—and those parkways were the only land where
people could grow food. Plus no one was being cited for the
discarded old toilets, couches and used condoms on the street—
but I got a citation for bringing nature, beauty, pride, art, and
a sense of peace and calm to the neighborhood. It just made
no sense.†

---

* Ron Finley, "A Guerilla Gardener in South Central LA," filmed February 2013,
TED video, 10:45, https://www.ted.com/talks/ron_finley_a_guerilla_gardener_in_south
_central_la.
† Ron Finley, "They Tried to Arrest Me for Planting Carrots," *Fortune*, February 25, 2015,
http://fortune.com/2015/02/25/they-tried-to-arrest-me-for-planting-carrots/.

Finley's defiance ultimately changed the law. The warrant was suspended after the *Los Angeles Times* reported on the case and a supportive petition was formed. In 2013, the city changed the law, making it legal to cultivate a garden in a city-owned parkway.

Mexican artist Pedro Reyes takes the "get gangsta with your shovel" motto to another level. In his ongoing project Palas por Pistolas (Shovels for Guns), which began in 2008, Reyes collected 1,527 guns from the violence-ridden town of Culiacán in western Mexico—one of the deadliest cities in the world. In collaboration with the botanical garden of Culiacán, Reyes arranged a program in which residents could exchange their guns for coupons that they could use to purchase home goods in local stores. The guns were then steamrolled, melted, and shaped into 1,527 shovels. These shovels are being given to arts institutions and public schools to plant 1,527 trees around the world.

Athleticism

The difference between actions and activities that focus on individual excellence—often at the expense of awesomeness—and those that focus on creative community building is important, and we can also see it in different forms of athletic activity.

Roughly since the 1960s new forms of awesome athletics—street skating (Rollerblading and skateboarding), BMX, breaking (or break dancing), certain forms of snowboarding and skiing, parkour, and others—have emerged. Obviously people do awe-inspiring things on skateboards, Rollerblades, skis, and snowboards—triple backflips, massive rail grinds, technical switch-ups, or giant switch quadruple underflip 1620s. But what makes these athletic pursuits "awesome" in our new sense?

To illustrate the difference between awesome athletics and non-awesome athletics, consider the difference between swimming (great but not awesome) and street skating (awesome). Most of us are familiar with the athletics of swimming. Individuals compete against one another in a small set of highly rule-governed matches. The International Swimming Federation (FINA) defines the rules for four primary styles: breaststroke, backstroke, butterfly, and freestyle (which defaults to front crawl, the fastest style). Swimmers, usually individuals but also teams and relay groups, train and compete to achieve the fastest times swimming in these styles. The results can be breathtaking, amazing, inspiring—individual swimmers can certainly be awesome. But on the whole the athletics of swimming are not governed by the ethics of awesomeness. The rules of swimming are very strict, the guidelines are absolutely clear, and nearly all creative or expressive deviations are strongly discouraged. Swimming is an especially vivid example here because the viewer can hardly see the individual athlete in the midst of so much splashing.

We tend to be less familiar with the athletics of street skating in its classical form. Or if we are familiar with it, we have a somewhat distorted view from focusing too much on televised spectacles, often competitions like the ESPN X Games. At its heart, street skating—and here I include the criminally under-appreciated and "uncool" sport of inline skating—is very different from swimming. The basic form of street skating involves a group of skaters who venture out into the city or suburban streets to various skate spots, often in search of something new—a new handrail to grind, a novel gap or stair set to jump, an unfamiliar ledge or curb to break in. Skaters seek to develop their talents and skills at these skate spots in a mutually appreciative environment of other skaters who (usually) know and encourage each other. One skater might be trying to invent a new trick; another might be trying to master a certain grind or board trick; a third might be trying to spin as she jumps down a set of stairs. Other skaters recognize these efforts and celebrate when the skater achieves her goal, which might take many, many tries and more than a few scrapes and bruises. The same celebratory, appreciative spirit is returned when the next skater lands his trick. The grand aim of all of this is the development of the skater's individual style and talent in a community of mutually appreciative and encouraging skaters. As a result, a premium is placed on innovation, creativity, and boldness to the near complete detriment of rule following—indeed, the only "rules" are those set by the physical limits of the board or blade and the imaginative limits of the skater. The grand aim is, in other words, awesomeness—the cultivation, expression, and appreciation of individuality in an active community of skaters.

When it comes to awesomeness, there are three salient differences between sports like swimming and those like street skating, and these differences track radically different approaches to human athletic activity.

The first difference concerns whether there is an emphasis on the cultivation of *individual style* or an emphasis on *competition*. These are not mutually exclusive. Some skaters have a competitive spirit, but competition—determining who is the best, the winner, the reigning champion—is not an essential element of the athletic activity. In fact, when it comes to skating, competitions rarely capture what is best about the sport and often force skaters into alien styles and awkward terrain.

It is fascinating that one of the most legendary moments in skate competition history was arguably not even part of a competition. At the 1999 ESPN X Games Tony Hawk was competing in the contest for best trick on a half-pipe (or "vert" ramp), along with fellow vert legends Andy Macdonald, Bob Burnquist, Bucky Lasek, and Neal Hendrix. Hawk decided that he was going to abandon the rules of competition and do whatever it took to land the elusive 900 (two and a half midair rotations)—a trick no one had landed and only few had even dared attempt. The other competitors knew what was at stake and encouraged him, cheering him on in a collective effort—pounding their skateboards on the coping, patting Hawk's back and helmet, and assuring him that he could do it.

After a series of falls, Hawk landed the 900 crouched but rolling, and there was a massive collective celebration. As he put it, "There has just been a general push for that trick to be done, and when someone does it, like, there's sort of a collective rejoicing."[*] Hawk's focus here is not exclusively on himself but on himself *as a skateboarder*, where being a skateboarder isn't just empty group cohesion but being a member of a coperson community. Landing the 900 was as much an achievement for skateboarding as it was for Hawk himself. That's because skating at its core is not about being the very best or collecting personal trophies and accolades. It's about style, creativity, and innovation. As Hawk puts it, his priorities do not lie in being a great competitor; his priority "has always been to be progressive. If I'm remembered as being progressive or as someone who broke limits—that's how I'd rather approach it."[†]

The second, related difference between sports like swimming and those like skating concerns whether there is an emphasis on the *mutual appreciation of individuality* or on *reverence for individual excellence*. Again, these are not mutually exclusive, but while both swimming and skating involve both of these things,

---

[*] "Tony Hawk 900," YouTube video, 1:51, from *Ultimate X: The Movie*, posted by "Zapatapro27," July 23, 2008, https://www.youtube.com/watch?v=e4QGnppJ-ys.
[†] Ibid.

they emphasize them in very different ways. Swimming is, in a sense, all about individual excellence. The whole point is to be the very best—to get the best time, set the record, garner the trophies and medals. Those who set the records are recognized as the definitive best. But most skaters don't really care about being the "absolute best"—whatever that would mean—when the emphasis is on style and community. This isn't to say that certain skaters are never regarded as standouts. There are obvious choices: Tony Hawk, Mark Gonzales, Rodney Mullen, Jon Julio, Alex Broskow, and Chris Haffey. But even the standouts are in a sense a matter of taste. Alex Broskow isn't among the best inline skaters of all time because he has a lot of sponsors, definitively holds some world record, or won a bunch of gold medals on TV. He's among the best because of his nearly perfect style, his grasp of a wide range of very difficult tricks, his innovative boldness, his insightful ability to find good skate spots, the arc of his career from his early days full of giant hammers (big, risky tricks) to the sheer precision and beauty of his later switch-ups, wheelies, and rails—the list could easily go on, and we could come up with equally impressive, though very different lists for Gonzales, Mullen, and Haffey. Whereas a great swimmer is like an amazingly refined machine, a great skater is like a stunning and dynamic work of art.

The third difference concerns whether there is an emphasis on *creativity and innovation* or an emphasis on *rule-following*. When it comes to swimming, excellence and rule adherence are inseparable. Any deviation from the rules and you are disqualified. Street skating, in contrast, is highly rule averse: There are no rules in street skating, and street skaters even have to abandon many rules and norms of public life. In order to find good tricks and new challenges, skaters need to cultivate an unusual perspective on the urban environment. The normal, rule-following public citizen sees stairs and thinks, "One walks up these"; he sees a handrail and understands that it affords holding and supports balance as one uses the stairs; he sees a planter and understands its usefulness for sitting and the definition of public space. Skaters abandon these norms and rules of public spatial orientation and find their own path through public space—handrails are opportunities for daring grinds; stairs, an opportunity to jump, flip, and spin. Even these descriptions will sound unbearably generic to a skater because what makes an urban space good for skating—much like what makes a subject good for painting—is a highly particular, individual matter that depends on who is considering it, when, and why. Not all stairs are good for jumping, and some that are good for jumping are even better for some other trick, maybe even something entirely unheard-of and specific to that site.

•

While street skating embodies the ethics of awesomeness, even the more rigid athletic activities can provide opportunities for rule breaking, creative innovation, and the expression of individuality.

Surya Bonaly is a French former figure skater who rose through the ranks of competitive figure skating in the late 1980s. By the early 1990s, she was ranking first in world-class competitions, beating the very best skaters in the world.*

But Bonaly wasn't your normal figure skater. Just before she began her free program at the 1994 World Figure Skating Championships (the Worlds), a TV announcer watching her skate onto the ice noticed that she was wearing different skates on each foot: "She's a very unusual skater, in every way," he said. "Everything about this girl is unusual."† According to sports journalist and commentator Christine Brennan, "She in many ways was the ultimate outsider, in a sport that you have to be an insider. I mean you really do have to play by the rules."‡

What made Bonaly so "unusual," the "ultimate outsider"? She is muscular and short—just over five feet one—but not small. She used her powerful legs to jump higher and skate faster than her competitors. Bonaly's skating was athletic, dynamic, quick, powerful; when she skated across the ice you heard force and energy.

This alone made her unusual, as her style stood in stark contrast

---

* The podcast *Radiolab* has a nice episode on Bonaly: http://www.radiolab.org/story/edge/.
† https://www.youtube.com/watch?v=fexLmuu4mlI.
‡ "Rebel on Ice," *Eva Longoria's Versus*, directed by Retta (2015), http://espn.go.com/video /clip?id=13416371.

to the "ideal" figure skater—the "ice princess." Ice-skating wasn't used to any style other than the lithe, light, and flowy (the word *graceful* was used a lot) movements of young ice princesses. The ice princess is smooth and elegant; when she skates across the ice it sounds light and pretty. It also *looks* light and pretty: Ice princesses often wear soft, light colors and skate to soft, light music. Bonaly wore flashy outfits and often chose unusual music. There was one more "rule" that she didn't observe: She is black. And although there had been successful black female skaters before Bonaly (US figure-skating champion and Olympic medalist Debi Thomas, for example), none had been quite as unusual as Bonaly.

Bonaly's style did not sit well with judges, who certainly recognized her superior athleticism and ability to jump, but who often said her skating lacked "artistry." Her technical scores were always higher than her scores in presentation. It seems that in the judges' minds Bonaly's aesthetics of power and verve couldn't compete with the traditional aesthetics of grace and prettiness. (Sports that so emphasize style can still suck when they accept only a single variety, which makes them preference dictators.)

By the '94 Worlds competition, the "unusual" Bonaly took her critics' views into consideration and changed her routine. The powerful jumps and technical skill were still on full display, but she had refined her artistic routine. One reporter notes these changes one year earlier:

Bonaly, 19, and her mother, Suzanne, have clearly adopted a more pragmatic attitude about getting the sort of notice that will translate to better scores. The hair was cut. ("Because the judges didn't like it," Suzanne Bonaly said.) For now, at least, there are no more vain attempts at quadruple jumps. . . . The skating costumes are simple. . . . A skater? Bonaly certainly looked like one earlier in the week, easily beating U.S. champion Nancy Kerrigan to win one of the two women's qualifying groups at the World Championships. Bonaly landed six triple jumps with grace, and the rest of her four-minute program had surprising aesthetic appeal.*

Bonaly retained her power but altered her presentation to appeal to the judges' preferences—her stunning routine at the 1994 Worlds put her in first place with only one competitor remaining, the Japanese ice princess Yuka Sato. Sato delivered, and when it came down to a decision, Bonaly narrowly lost the gold medal to her in a 5-4 vote. She expressed her outrage by refusing to stand on the podium. With confusion on her face and tears in her eyes, she told a reporter, "I guess I'm just not lucky."

In the years that followed, the judges' preferences would not change, and despite her many high performances and

---

* Phil Hersh, "Bonaly's Plan for Revenge: This Time, Keep It Simple," March 12, 1993, *Chicago Tribune*, http://articles.chicagotribune.com/1993-03-12/sports/9303191274_1_suzanne-bonaly-surya-bonaly-woman-skater.

achievements, Bonaly never won an Olympic or World gold medal (despite three consecutive second-place finishes in the Worlds).

Bonaly's final amateur competition was the 1998 Winter Olympics in Nagano, Japan. She finished sixth in her barely flawed short program, and some argue that she deserved fifth place, that this was yet another example of bias against her. However, she was skating with a serious injury—a recently ruptured Achilles tendon—and she knew she couldn't manage a gold-winning long program. So when she approached the ice, she was determined to finally and definitively show the judges what she thought of their rules and exclusive aesthetic standards.

Bonaly's technical skill allowed her to do something no other female figure skater could do: *backflips*. Backflips were (and still are) illegal in competition because, as the justification goes, they are extremely dangerous. But so are triple salchows and quadruple toe loops. Even more damning of the backflip, though, is the rule that all jumps must be landed on one foot, and this was unheard of—even unthinkable—with a backflip. But it wasn't unthinkable to Bonaly. Near the end of her routine she picked up speed, turned around, and did a backflip, landing backward perfectly on one foot. To cap it off, she did the splits in midair, upside down. She finished her routine and turned her back to the judges.

Bonaly demonstrates how clever and courageous awesomeness can be. If you're bold enough, you can be awesome even in highly rule-governed, restrictive, conservative, oppressive conditions. Her awesomeness challenged figure skating's prevailing ideal; her physical mastery, daring, and norm-breaking style helped create a new community of skaters and a broader perspective on what makes a figure skater good. She inspired the next generation of young skaters and helped push the sport in a more stylistically diverse and appreciative direction.

Civic Life

We also see awesomeness in creative and communal approaches to civic life—to our lives as citizens in public. Earlier we considered how the first rule of improv acting, *Yes! And . . .* , can help us understand what it is to be game. When you combine the spirit of improv with collective action and public awareness you can generate awesomeness.

Consider founder Charlie Todd's group Improv Everywhere. This self-described "prank collective" specializes in "creating scenes of chaos and joy in public spaces." As the group describes itself, "Improv Everywhere is, at its core, about having fun. We're big believers in 'organized fun.' . . . We get satisfaction from coming up with an awesome idea and making it come to life. In the process we hopefully bring excitement to otherwise unexciting locales and give strangers a unique experience and a great story to tell."*

* "FAQ," Improv Everywhere, http://improveverywhere.com/faq/.

One of their "awesome ideas" was realized in Frozen Grand Central. More than two hundred "agents" simultaneously froze in place in Grand Central's main concourse, as busy New Yorkers rushed through. Some were in the middle of eating a banana; others had just dropped papers or were on the phone—they all stopped what they were doing and stood motionless for five minutes. A mystified and fascinated audience quickly developed to study the frozen crowd. When the actors simultaneously resumed their activities, the audience erupted in applause.* The word *awesome* is used to describe the event scores upon scores of times in YouTube comments.†

Another one of their influential awesome ideas is High Five Escalator, first realized in 2009. During the morning rush, the improv collective went to the 53rd and Lex subway station in New York City, where there are two giant escalators that carry thousands of commuters from deep underground to the upper levels. Right next to the escalators is a staircase that no one uses because it's so long—especially when you're just trying to get to work. Six Improv Everywhere agents stood on the staircase as throngs of commuters ascended past them on the escalator. The first five held a series of signs. The first one the commuters saw read ROB WANTS, then TO GIVE YOU, then A HIGH FIVE! and then

---

* "Frozen Grand Central," Improv Everywhere, http://improveverywhere.com/2008/01/31/frozen-grand-central/.
† Including a comment from Madhav Shrestha, "This is what 'AWESOME' means. Hats off!!!!."

GET READY! The fifth and final sign read ROB, with an arrow pointing down to a man with his hand up in perfect high-five form.* As they figured out what was happening, commuters smiled, laughed, and delivered resounding high fives.

High Five Escalator used the high five to poke holes in the script of the morning commute and create a little social opening. You don't necessarily need a large group to pull something like this off, however, as Nathaniel Kassel proved in 2007† and Meir Kalmanson proved in 2014 with his project High Five New York. New York City is full of people hailing cabs with outstretched arms and who, with a little imagination, appear to be in need of a high five. As Kalmanson says in an interview, "I'm all about human connection and I believe the high five is a simple yet friendly way of showing someone, 'Hey, let's be friends.' When I was walking in Manhattan and looked at all the people who were hailing cabs, all I saw were men and women being left hanging from a perfect high five."‡

Kalmanson ran around giving high fives to all the people he saw as "being left hanging"—from businessmen and -women to shoppers, tourists, the youthful, and the elderly (Kassel used a

---

* "High Five Escalator," Improv Everywhere, http://improveverywhere.com/2009/02/09 /high-five-escalator/.
† "High Five New York City," YouTube video, 4:20, posted by "natek213," July 31, 2009, https://www.youtube.com/watch?v=QMQk8Uncl9k.
‡ Dmitry Belyaev, "Interview: Metro Chats with Filmmaker Meir Kalmanson, Man Behind 'High-Five New York,'" *Metro*, October 10, 2014, http://www.metro.us/entertainment /interview-metro-chats-with-filmmaker-meir-kalmanson-man-behind-high-five-new-york /tmWniD---16nm5q6V1Go0/.

bike to do the same). In nearly every case people initially respond with a little surprise and then with a giant smile.

These public actions engage broad human sentiments—ones that form the core of nearly everyone's individuality: the appreciation of kindness; the fun of play; joy; the feeling you get when you high-five someone. But other awesome public actions engage rarer, less universal, or more local or challenging thoughts, emotions, and ideals.

Over eleven months in 1979 artist Mierle Laderman Ukeles shook the hands of every New York City sanitation worker—all eighty-five hundred of them across five boroughs—thanking them for their essential and nearly universally underappreciated work. This performance piece, titled *Touch Sanitation*, serves as a reminder of the enormous service these men and women perform for us every day (specifically, collecting more than 10,500 tons of garbage and 1,760 tons of recyclables every single day*). But it does more than animate our connection to strangers—it revives a specific sense of sanitation workers' value, of the worth of their work as laborers. It opens our minds to and transforms our normal thoughts about the kinds of labor we tend to avoid thinking about, but without which society couldn't function.†

---

* New York City Department of Sanitation, "About DSNY," City of New York, http://www1.nyc.gov/assets/dsny/about/inside-dsny.shtml.

† For a kind of encyclopedia of creative public actions, some of which are awesome and some of which are not, see Nato Thompson and Gregory Sholette's *The Interventionists: Users' Manual for the Creative Disruption of Everyday Life* (North Adams, MA: Mass MoCA, 2006). Also relevant are Doris Sommer's *The Work of Art in the World: Civic Agency and Public Humanities* (Durham, NC: Duke University Press, 2014) and Diana Boros's *Creative Re-*

Art

Many of the creative community builders we have discussed so far are either artists or think of their works and lives in terms of art: Mockus, Haaning, Reyes, Finley, Fazlalizadeh, Ukeles, and others. Awesome art is the art of social openings—of creating, cultivating, and encouraging them, but also of performing, theatricalizing, depicting, and representing them. We have already encountered hints and examples of awesome art; now it's time to take a closer look.

The paradigm of art as we tend to understand it today is object centered (a painting, sculpture, installation, etc.), expressively one-sided (the artist expresses herself to you through the object), nonparticipatory (you receive and interpret her expression), and caught up in art world institutions like galleries, museums, and art fairs. Awesome art, in contrast, is paradigmatically interpersonal, process or interaction oriented, expressively dynamic, and social or participatory.* Consider what emerged from the recent and massive global street art movement. Artistic graffiti began in the 1970s in the streets of New York City and Philadelphia. Talented writers controversially illuminated their city streets with colorful, highly stylized, and

---

bellion for the Twenty-First Century: The Importance of Public and Interactive Art to Political Life in America (New York: Palgrave Macmillan, 2012).

* Of course, more traditional artworks can also be awesome, but they tend not to highlight or emphasize awesomeness in the same way.

often illegal lettering and pop graphics, using the city walls, trains, and sidewalks as their canvas. Although the timing is hard to pinpoint, by the mid- to late 1990s, graffiti culture had expanded into something new—something people started calling "street art," where the street was being regularly used for art in a revolutionary and awesome way.*

Many of us walk down the streets of our towns and cities paying no mind to potential social openings. We use our streets as practical spaces that allow us to get from one place to another. And as we walk down the street, our minds are often on what we have to do, where we have to go, or what more generally is happening in our lives. We might be listening to music or looking at something on our phones. We aren't in the moment, tend not to notice details, and generally ignore the people around us.

But by the mid-1990s, a movement to challenge this was clearly underway, with artists exploring the many ways we can alter the aesthetics of the street. They began innovating with new ways of using the street for art, calling attention to our common spaces and collective lives in ways that animate both.

Street art pioneer Leon Reid IV noticed that by tweaking street signs he could personalize them, and thereby personalize the street. Others, like Bruno Taylor, noticed that bus stops were cold and impersonal, so they installed swings to make

---

* This is not to say that artistic graffiti cannot be awesome. For a clear example see the artist MOMO's "Manhattan Tag" (2006). MOMO created a mysterious path through the city by tagging his name in a thin line of paint across the entire width of Manhattan.

them more dynamic and fun. Some beautified the urban land-scape to make it more inviting and homely. Artist C. Finley aesthetically altered the street by covering urban Dumpsters with vibrant wallpaper, suggesting that even these ugly deni-zens of the street can reflect our common life. Others turned unused phone booths into free libraries with a "take one, leave one" policy. Still others made street signs and crosswalks more play-ful by altering them in a way that makes pedestrians smile and point out what they have found to other pedestrians. The artist stikman places small yellow thermoplastic stickmen in the mid-dle of crosswalks; the French artist Invader "invades" cities, plac-ing mosaic space invaders around the city for people to seek out and discover.

We can gain a deeper understanding of the awesomeness of street art by thinking more about what the street is. It is com-mon to treat the street as simply a logistical space, one that fa-cilitates travel from one place to another. But the "street" in street art is different from this. The street is a public cultural space that, ideally, facilitates self-expression and the kind of mutual recognition that public expression enables. The street in this sense is a place to express oneself, and to recognize and appreciate one another. As such, it is a locus of life and commu-nity for cities and towns.

This cultural notion of the street gives it a certain energy and status: It doesn't just allow us to get from one place to another—it allows us to express ourselves, and to acknowledge and appreciate each other as individuals. It's a place where we can publicly flaunt our style and declare our commitments and values, where we can see and be seen for who we are or aspire to be. As the great cultural critic and theorist of urban life William Whyte says, "The street is the river of life for the city. We come to these places not to escape, but to partake of it."* This is not to deny that, as we have noted, some street spaces are highly conflicted places, dangerous and oppressive even to those who should be able to claim them as their own. But these are distortions of the street that art can help reshape and revive (as we saw with Fazlalizadeh's art in chapter 3).

Understanding the street in this way helps us understand what street art is and why it is important. Street art is art that uses the cultural street as a medium. Street artists use the street by taking its cultural function and enhancing, repairing, highlighting, or cultivating it.[†]

Street artists are discovering ways of creating awesome community by toying with the norms of the street in a way that creates a truly awesome public space. Their artworks transform the neglected spaces of the street; they draw our attention to the ways we habitually treat, or rather ignore, these spaces. We ignore them just as we tend to ignore each other when we're walking through

---

* See his film *The Social Life of Small Urban Spaces* (1980).

† I develop this way of thinking about street art and consider its place in art history in two papers: "Street Art: The Transfiguration of the Commonplaces," *Journal of Aesthetics and Art Criticism* 68, no. 3 (2010): 243–57; and "Using the Street for Art: A Reply to Baldini," *Journal of Aesthetics and Art Criticism* 74, no. 2 (2016): 191–5.

our towns and cities. Street art is being used to awaken us to the possibilities of a truly shared public space, one that treats its denizens not as mere inhabitants but as individuals.

Street artists achieve this by making the street a locus of individual expression and exploration; they make it visually interesting and more inviting, turning it into a game, making it homelier, more comfortable, or more playful, or giving it a voice to speak about social, political, or cultural issues. In a project called the Comfy City, artists Jane Tsong and Robert Powers turn abandoned Los Angeles tree stumps into sidewalk seats. Cities and towns often cut down overgrown sidewalk trees and leave ugly, aging stumps in their wake. Tsong and Powers carve them into seats and invite others to relax or do the same:

> Please have a seat. Or make one. Our urban spaces could definitely benefit from more public seating and relaxation. How luxurious it will seem when we are able to rest our feet where we please once in a while. Let us know the location of other stumps in need of improvement. Or for the handy and brave, a chain saw can do the job with two careful cuts. Ask your local tool rental shop for safety tips. Let us make the comfy city ours.*

Sure, there are park benches and city-designed resting spots, but Tsong and Powers invite us to consider the municipal and public

---

* "The Comfy City," Jane Tsong and Robert Powers, http://www.myriadsmallthings.org /comfycity.html.

attitude toward our shared space. Why just cut the tree down and leave a gross reminder of lost glory? Why not make a seat?

Creative and communal attitudes toward public space are evident in more ambitious projects. Amar Bakshi's *Portals* is a public art project aimed at transforming local public spaces into global public spaces primed for interpersonal appreciation. A "portal" is a shipping container painted gold, equipped with immersive audio and video technology, and placed in a public space. The technology presents a hologram-like image and audio of a live life-size person standing in a distant portal—one that could be in Jerusalem, Bulawayo, Progreso, Isfahan, or Los Angeles. All portals are connected to one another. As you enter the global street space, you can look this person in the eye, see them smile, start a conversation, or even sing, dance, or play music together.

Bakshi notes how his portals enhance public space. "Portals as an initiative is really about creating a space that has some indeterminacy to its purpose, which I think is like another way of saying, to create a public space," he says. "A small addition to an existing public space can open up a whole range of new uses that I think both vitalize the space in new ways, but also help revitalize it the way it currently is. It sparks that dialog locally, and programmatically it creates ideas across institutions, and I think really strengthens the public space."*

---

* "Next City: Gold-Painted Shipping Containers Create a Global Public Space," Shared_ Studios, http://www.sharedstudios.com/press-list/2016/5/11/next-city-gold-painted-shipping -containers-create-a-global-public-space.

One portal project focuses on discussions about social justice and connects Newark, New Jersey, with Milwaukee,
Wisconsin—two US cities that struggle with extremely high
incarceration rates among black men. The portals connect these
communities so they can talk about their struggles, safety,
and coping and community-building strategies, among other
things. Collaborator and cosponsor Dr. Rod K. Brunson, dean
of Rutgers School of Criminal Justice, notes, "What we've
found is people have these very rich and detailed and passionate
conversations with strangers."* This captures the very point of
the project—to publicly cultivate these kinds of connections
through dialogue, shared experience, music making, dancing,
and so on.†

•

Portals, street art, and tree stump chairs are, in many ways, of
a piece with an art movement whose initial rise roughly coin-
cides with the rise of artistic graffiti (1970s) and took off with
the rise of street art (1990s). Variably referred to as "social practice," "relational aesthetics," "dialogical aesthetics," or perhaps

---

* David Porter, "Experimental Installations Put the Social in Social Science," Phys.org,
May 30, 2016, http://phys.org/news/2016-05-experimental-social-science.html#jCp.
† For another project that focuses on cultivating dialogue between disparate groups, see
Suzanne Lacy's *The Roof Is On Fire*, which ran in Oakland, California, from 1993 to 1994.

most broadly "participatory art," these works attempt to make art out of social life.*

Once we understand what it is to have an "art" of the street, where "the street" is understood as a site for a certain kind of interpersonal expression and connection, we can see the potential for a more general art of human social life. The art of the street is one that enables and activates the street—the public cultural space wherein we express, recognize, and appreciate one another. We can abstract from the focus on the street as a locus of art to see the potential for an art of human social relations in general. In the past few decades, we see a clear focus on social connection in art production; a growing wave of creative projects seek to create, cultivate, perform, or represent social life.

Consider Tino Sehgal's *This Progress*, which took place at the Guggenheim Museum in New York City in 2010. In this piece participants were led by a guide or "interpreter" as they walked up the spiraling ramp of the Frank Lloyd Wright rotunda, whose white walls were entirely stripped of art. The interpreters were volunteers of all ages whom Sehgal worked with in creating the piece. The first one you'd meet was a child of no more than ten years old who'd ask you what you think

---

* I am grateful for and indebted to two outstanding art history books that discuss such artworks. For many more examples, details, and discussion, see Grant Kester's *Conversation Pieces: Community and Communication in Modern Art* (Berkeley: University of California Press, 2004) and Claire Bishop's *Artificial Hells: Participatory Art and the Politics of Spectatorship* (Brooklyn, NY: Verso, 2012).

progress is. The child would probe your answer and engage you in a discussion until you were handed off to a high school student, who continued to ask questions about progress and explore your replies. Then you would be handed off to someone in their thirties, who would ostensibly shift the topic away from progress—to travel, family, happiness, career. Finally, you would be introduced to someone in late middle age who would continue the discussion, complicating the question of progress until the end, when they would say, "The piece is called *This Progress.*"

Like much of Sehgal's art, *This Progress* embodies the ethics of awesomeness and puts the dynamics of social openings on display by merging perfect strangers who dialogue with, learn about, challenge, and appreciate one another. As Lauren Collins writes in her *New Yorker* profile of Sehgal, "He is, in a sense, an architect of interaction. His works are collaborations, new builds on human turf."* The "new builds" Sehgal's piece constructs are moments of connection, insight, and shared joy. *New York* magazine art critic Jerry Saltz writes, "This show is wondrous-strange, and can produce waves of uncanny self-revelation, surprise, and delight."†

Sehgal's work is deliberately opposed to much of the suckiness of art-world culture. His pieces are not commodifiable objects

---

* Lauren Collins, "The Question Artist," *The New Yorker*, August 6, 2012.
† Jerry Saltz, "How I Made an Artwork Cry," *New York*, February 7, 2010.

meant for decoration or status; instead he orchestrates impermanent human interactions and interventions but then steps aside. He famously disallows documentation of his work—no catalogs, press releases, photographs, or even paper trails of sales. He also toys with the competitive art market. At the Art Basel art fair in 2004, Sehgal made the two galleries that represent him—and so compete with each other—stand next to each other and allowed them to speak only one word at a time. To form sentences in attempts to discuss and sell his works, the gallery representatives had to work together, alternating each word.* Sehgal's producer, Asad Raza, notes how Sehgal is influenced by his skateboarding past: "I think a lot of Tino's stuff comes from skateboarders looking at railings and concrete, and thinking, How can I use that in a different way?"†

Another whose work focuses on social life is British artist Stephen Willats, a venerable practitioner of awesome art. One could choose almost any of Willats's artworks from the past forty-five years: *Meta Filter* (1973), his Multiple Clothing series (1965–1999), *The Kids Are in the Streets* (1982).‡ In a work titled *Brentford Towers*, Willats collaborated with residents of a West London apartment complex. He was not alone in seeing the domineering beige towers as "monumental objects" that

---

* The piece is called *This Is Competition*.
† Collins, "The Question Artist."
‡ It's notable that Willats was quick to recognize the "special world" one can construct with friends through skateboarding. *The Kids Are in the Streets* is about how kids use skateboarding to resist the suckiness of life in a tower block in South London.

"seemed to deny the complexity of people's lives within it."* To address this, Willats worked with the residents to construct a communal sense of presence for their individual lives. He interviewed them about their living spaces and asked them to choose a meaningful object from their living rooms. They then discussed the importance of this object and how it relates to something outside of the residential tower. Willats used this information to create a visual artwork that displayed the resident, the tower, the interior object, and the exterior object, with lines connecting each and a quote from the resident about their life at Brentford Towers. These works were displayed on each floor of the building, giving other residents insight into their neighbors' lives and creating a richer and more visible community of individuals who live there. Such communities are central to Willats's art: "My work engages the audience in a new way of encountering art in society. I am not talking about a compliance, but something more active, a mutual understanding, an interaction between people—similar to the dynamic image of the homeostat where all the parts of the network are equal and equally linked."†

As art historian and critic Claire Bishop notes, it is not clear how we should think about these social artworks. They seem to be works of ethics or social politics *and* works of art. When critics move to understand and assess them, they often turn to

---

* *A State of Agreement*, directed by Charlotte Ginsborg (2008).
† "Context," Stephen Willats, http://stephenwillats.com/context/.

ethical ways of thinking—empathy, identification, community, social and personal transformation—while at the same time insisting that these works are art and as such are properly compared with other works of art rather than with social or political initiatives intended to bolster community.* The difficulty about how to think of these creative works seems slightly deeper than even this, for I think there is a strong inclination to say that many of them are *beautiful*. They are not just artworks with social intent; they are exemplary works of beauty. If that's right, then we are especially stuck: We want to say that these social works are artworks, that some are even beautiful artworks, but that their value lies squarely in their creatively social, community-building character.†

The problem is that we are wedged firmly between the categories of ethics and aesthetics. The solution is that these works are not exactly ethical and they are not exactly aesthetic—they are a new combination of both, or a new thing with elements of both. They're awesome. The themes, innovations, strategies,

---

* See Bishop's book *Artificial Hells*, p. 19. Art historian, critic, and curator Grant Kester attempts to make sense of these works in terms of the "creative orchestration of dialogical exchange" (*Conversation Pieces*, p. 189), in which dialogical exchange "requires that we strive to acknowledge the specific identity of our interlocutors and conceive of them not simply as subjects on whose behalf we might act but as co-participants in the transformation of both self and society" (p. 79).

† These artworks also challenge us to rethink our understanding of beauty. For an attempt to do so, see my "On the Interest in Beauty and Disinterest," in *Philosophers' Imprint*, June 2016, vol. 16, no. 9, pp. 1–14. All articles in *Philosophers' Imprint* are available for free online. This one is here: http://quod.lib.umich.edu/p/phimp/3521354.0016.009/1.

and reception of much contemporary art, especially street art and social practice, are in significant ways manifestations of this general cultural ethos—one that informs far more than socially minded art practices and includes political innovations, approaches to athletics, modes of everyday social interaction, visions of social and public life, and personal style.

Watch Out

Note that I'm not saying that you have to be so bold, creatively altruistic, awesomely artistic, or beautifully risky to be awesome. Being an excellent social artist is not as simple as, say, mimicking Stephen Willats. A good amount of participatory art is misguided (if well intended) and a lot of the good social practice works are good because they are shocking, disturbing, even perverse; they exhibit artistic values other than awesomeness. Not every Awesome Foundation project is awesome, and there are other forms of charity and activism that excellently promote and embody the ethics of awesomeness. A good amount of street art is destructive, messy, or pointless; some of Improv Everywhere's machinations are not awesome.* Being awesome is not as easy as learning to ollie or put together a sweet outfit.

But sometimes it can seem that way because of how

---

* Some of their missions are true pranks that deceive people in sucky ways.

awesomeness is represented to us via television, YouTube, social media, advertising, and so on. Just under the surface of the story we have told in this chapter lies an important warning, one reflected in a lesson we can learn from the cultural trajectory of *cool*. Each practice discussed here is threatened by click-hungry ad agencies, marketing companies, television and media corporations, competition promoters, news companies, and culture hucksters who make us think awesomeness is easy, or disconnected from our daily lives, or just a matter of having an epic night out, wearing sunglasses onstage, or winning an X Games medal. Our enthusiasm for the kind of connection and culture that awesomeness fosters is all too easily exploited, televised, recorded, and made into a spectacle that threatens to turn awesomeness into something that we simply stare at, share on social media, and move on. These shifts to cultures of spectacle and easy entertainment really suck. Not because all spectacles suck—that's obviously false—but because they tend to have a sucky influence on already-awesome activities. They turn skate culture into televised competition culture; charity into self-promotion; street art into social media strategies. The result is that awesome inspiration moves us to click our way into a YouTube rabbit hole rather than get up and get out. Skate culture, street and social art, awesome forms of altruism and civic life—they are all changed when they become things to merely watch and react to rather than things to engage in, be inspired by, and act on in our everyday lives.

That might seem a little ironic because so much social media marketing—and, more generally, so much enthusiasm about the democratizing promise of the Internet—tries to harness the allure of awesomeness by promising to reinforce and cultivate social bonds. Mark Zuckerberg often states his admirable desire to "connect the whole world"—not just to the Internet, but as citizens, friends, family, and loved ones. As good as such connection is, it comes with a price.* We are often compromised in our digital lives, tempted into being fake-ass people, braggarts, blowhards, half-assers, or simply sucky. The image is all too familiar: several friends sitting in a restaurant, all looking at their phones and ignoring each other. Or, you're in a conversation with someone and the moment he's done talking he ignores your response to check his texts, shoot off a tweet, or see whether anyone "likes" his status update. Or a half-asser leaves their phone on the table during your meet-up and distractedly glances at it every time it flashes, buzzes, or pings. We too often feel a persistent, nagging suspicion that there's something a little more interesting to do or look at on our phones. We can really suck if we focus too much of our cultural activity around the digital opportunities that social media and the Internet supply.

---

* For a refreshing counterweight to unchecked optimism about the Internet see Astra Taylor, *The People's Platform: Taking Back Power and Culture in the Digital Age* (New York: Metropolitan Books, 2014).

This isn't to say that social media is all bad, or that Zuckerberg-style aspirations are entirely misguided—quite the opposite—and no doubt Facebook, YouTube, Instagram, and similar companies have played an important role in generating and facilitating awesomeness. Such aspirations are another expression of the hold that awesomeness has on us and of the promise of new technology to help us really connect. When used in the right way, social media and new technology can help us cultivate the awesomeness we aspire to. A case in point: Consider the messaging app and art project Somebody, a social opening generator created by artist, filmmaker, and writer Miranda July. When you send a message to a friend using Somebody, your message is not delivered directly to your friend but to the Somebody user nearest to them, who then has the opportunity to find your friend and deliver the message.* Or consider hitchBOT, a robot created to hitchhike through various countries, relying entirely on friendly strangers to move it along the right path. The robot cannot move, but it can converse and tell you about itself, its favorites pastimes, and its desire to visit various monuments, artworks, and historical sites. In an enormously sucky turn of events, after successful trips through Canada, Germany, and the Netherlands,

---

* The app is currently defunct. More information is available here: http://somebody app.com/.

hitchBOT was destroyed on its US tour one late night in Philadelphia.*

There is a lot of work to do to make social media, new technology, and the Internet more generally, truly awesome, especially considering the growing amount of fake, click-bait content—throwaway videos, "news" articles, vapid music—created to distract, advertise, persuade, and sell. As former Facebook data scientist Jeff Hammerbacher tells us, fake-assery animates so much social media development, which is often aimed more at selling products than connecting people: "The best minds of my generation are thinking about how to make people click ads. That sucks."† Indeed it does.

The awesome practices discussed here are so much more than entertaining visuals and shareable content; through these social, personal, and cultural achievements—whether they're large or small, lasting or fleeting—we can glimpse the outlines of a new social culture. They give us insight into the ways awesomeness is shaping how we give, play, explore, and create, and they illustrate the desire and potential for real awesomeness in our collective spaces, our group activities, our artworks, our daily lives, and our very selves. In addition to being technically

---

* Information about hitchBOT and its successors is available here: http://mir1.hitch bot.me/.

† Ashlee Vance, "This Tech Bubble Is Different," *Bloomberg*, April 14, 2011, https://www .bloomberg.com/news/articles/2011-04-14/this-tech-bubble-is-different.

awesome, they promote the ethics of awesomeness by promoting the various concerns, character traits, activities, and habits that make us awesome and not sucky. And they point the way to greater awesomeness in other human pursuits: business, medicine, education, and management, among others. Together, they provide a vivid alternative to bleak visions of a sucky society and show us how we can strengthen and focus our hope.

Chapter 7

Becoming Awesome

BECOMING AWESOME CAN seem overwhelming. Sure, you start with yourself—you think, "How can I be more awesome?" You do a few more awesome things more often. But then you think: "What about my community of friends, my partner, or my family?" You reach out and foster communal awesomeness, building more awesome connections and reaching out to some new copeople. Soon you go bold and cultivate a more awesome civic presence. But surely you could improve on this—many of these things are fleeting, after all—so you decide to take it to the next level. Maybe you create an awesome artwork or get involved in an awesome charity. But then what? Couldn't you be even more awesome? You need to work harder. It starts to seem like the most awesome thing you can do is drop everything and spread awesomeness as far and wide as possible. Maybe you should run for office, become a full-time "awesome" artist, or write a whole book trying to convince your sistren and brethren of the awesomeness of awesomeness. But who wants to do that? Surely there are other important things to do and values to pursue. And won't you kinda suck if you spend so much time obsessing over awesomeness? (I worry about that.) It starts to sound like becoming awesome is self-defeating.

Although that's a natural way to think about it, it's not the right way. In fact, this line of thought evinces a slightly sucky way of thinking—one that is all too easy to fall into, especially if we make the mistake of thinking of creative community builders as people to imitate now and again rather than as people whose insights, strategies, and styles can shape our lives. Truly awesome people don't ask, "How can I *be* more awesome?" They ask, "What can I *do* to create more awesomeness?" Notice the difference: The latter, unlike the former, is not about how you can gain some status or embody some value. Rather, it's about what you can contribute to the collective realization of value (awesomeness)—even when that value might not inhere squarely in *you*, but instead in your community, neighborhood, workplace, crew, or family. The answer to the second question clearly includes being down, game, chill, and generally non-sucky. Another way to put this point is: The advice "Be awesome!" is misleading, for being awesome is a *way* of doing things and not a thing to do. Focus instead on the more awkward advice: "Do [x] awesomely!" Or perhaps "Awesomize!" In other words, the first step in becoming awesome is, in a way, to forget about awesomeness as such and focus on doing what you do awesomely. It's not a goal but a result of doing the right things in the right way.

Of course, that doesn't make becoming awesome any easier. In fact, becoming awesome is even more obscure than this; it would be manageable if we knew exactly what it took to do things awesomely. However, while we can use our discussion to craft a rough guide, we can't hope for much detail because there's no recipe for doing the right things in the awesome way. There's a straightforward argument for this: If there were a recipe for awesomeness, then we could be awesome just by following it. But then you'd just have to follow the script of awesomeness—being awesome would be no different than being a normal coffee shop customer. Every NBA halftime would have a Jeremy Fry; every baseball team could expect a Glenn Burke; every subway escalator would have a Rob. As a result, there wouldn't be any creative community building because there would be nothing to create, no norms to break or scripts to innovate with. It would be scripts all the way down. Even worse, there wouldn't be any community building of the awesome variety because inveterate script followers are not "individuals in pursuit of the individual."

In other words, it would suck if there were a recipe for awesomeness. As our discussion reveals, there's nothing normal about awesomeness. It's essentially unusual. It is part of the very nature of awesomeness that it is creatively attentive to particular situations—to particular people and places, to the norms governing those people and places, and to the potential for creative community building. But this means that awesome's cleverness also makes it elusive, a matter of trial and error, something each person must cultivate for themselves.

Even within these constraints our theory can guide us—there are a few things we can say about what it takes to become more awesome.

·

If we want to embody and be surrounded by more awesomeness, then there is work to do at every level of social organization, from the grand scale of how we design our institutions, our cities, our companies, and our laws, to the smaller scale of how we tend to interact with others—with strangers, copeeps, and weird kids acting like Bon Jovi at halftime. The future of awesome comes down to who we aspire to be in our own lives and whether we want awesome style to be reflected in the world through the actions we perform, the individuals we create and cocreate, and the institutions we support.

If your goal in developing yourself, living your life, running a business, or leading a people is to be the number one, or the richest, or the most powerful person in the world, there's a good chance you suck. Possibly quite a lot. Why? Because in focusing all of your time, thought, and energy on being number one, you care too much about yourself alone to care about being awesome. To put it bluntly, you're probably an asshole, a self-promoter, a fake-ass person, a blowhard, a braggart, a douche-bag, or a thunder stealer. Being awesome requires us to think of and inspire others; it requires us to pay sympathetic, perceptive, and creative attention to people and situations, and you can't do that if, for all you really care, there's no one else around. If you're living a life, developing a style, becoming the kind of person who aims to make people laugh, think, play, imagine, smile, care, strive, or empathize, then you're probably attuned to the ethics of awesomeness.

So which one is it? Does the spirit of awesomeness flow within you? Does it flow within your community or society? Here are some questions you can ask yourself to figure out where things stand:

1. Where do you belong on the Taxonomy of Awesome-ness and Suckiness? If you're having trouble answering this question, then consider this: In studying the dia-gram, you probably thought, "I totally know someone who is [wack, simply sucky, a blowhard, a braggart, etc.]." How do you compare to this person? What makes you more awesome or sucky? Why don't you belong on the same branch?

2. When was the last time you created a social opening? Do you ever really talk with your café people, grocer, or bartender? Why not? Is tonight's dinner the same as usual? Did you just throw on whatever shirt was clean and close? When was the last time you sent someone a gift just because, or went out of your way to tell someone that they were doing an awesome job?

3. What did you do the last time you were presented with a social opening? Were you sucky? Wack? Bored in the heart of the multitude? Or were you game?

4. How's your symmetry in the ethics of awesomeness? Do you always take up social openings but never create them yourself? Or do you always create social openings but never take them up?

5. When you did create or respond to a social opening, how did it go? Did it work? Did you unearth a coperson? Did you create a social opening for someone who is different from you, perhaps a person of a different race or sexuality? Did you take one up when someone of a different race or background offered one?

6. What can you do to create social openings? What skills can you deploy? Can you spontaneously dance, barter, invent a handshake, make art, build something, sing, cook a feast, forage, throw an inviting and fun party, notice and discuss beauty or style, fall in love

with a cuisine, a band, or a city, plan an epic hike or
road trip?

7. When was the last time you exercised your pure individuality? When was the last time you were silly,
broke the rules, or simply played?

8. Do you feel moved to do any of these things?

9. Do you have an awesome role model? Who is it and
why do they speak to you? If you don't, why not? Do
your role models suck?

10. Maybe you are pretty awesome, but what about your
community, culture, and society?

•

That should give you a rough idea of where to set your sights in
becoming awesome. But now let's think about more concrete
ways to achieve this. One way is to develop various habits and
abilities that help us succeed in creating and responding to social openings. We can think more about the creative community builders discussed in chapter 3, study them further, and
seek out our own exemplars of awesome. We can take into account the notes in chapter 4 on motivation and management in
the ethics of awesomeness and apply them to ourselves and our
social lives.

We can also consider a general lesson from our discussion of awesome culture. Reflecting on awesome altruism teaches us to be creative in our altruistic and charitable acts, from the foundations and nonprofits we support to how we give to our friends, neighbors, and communities. In considering awesome athletics, we might think about which of our activities embody the ethics of awesomeness and to what extent. How much of what you do and are promotes the cultivation of style, mutual appreciation of individuality, and innovation in contrast with competition, individual excellence, and rule following? Considering awesome civic life can inspire us to bring a more playful, creative, grateful, and perceptive attitude to our lives in public. And keeping an eye out for awesome art can give us new opportunities for social openings, can inspire new ideas for crew building, and can maintain our connection to the beauty and aesthetic excellence that fuels the ethics of awesomeness.

Putting these pieces together: Awesome culture gives us a picture of a person who is creatively generous, egalitarian, nonconformist, socially curious, open, innovative, cooperative, playful, and sympathetically attentive to individual style. It also gives us an image of activities, pursuits, and forms of society that embody and encourage these qualities. Do you and the people you know fit this picture? How much or how little? What about your crew or community? Your society?

Learning these lessons from awesome culture requires exercising and developing a range of underlying skills. More generally, we have to cultivate our social imaginations and excel at perceiving, interpreting, understanding, and sympathizing with our copeople.

Being good at creating social openings requires sensitivity to the reasons your existing or potential copeople have for and against taking up the opportunities. If your friend is a vegan, then don't surprise her with your very own venison jerky. That's obvious, but it's easy to overlook the subtler ways we can attend to our copeople. We have to be as perceptive as Constantin Guys: "If a fashion or the cut of a garment has been slightly modified, if bows and *chignons* have dropped a fraction towards the nape of the neck, if waists have been raised and skirts have become fuller, be very sure that his eagle eye will already have spotted it from however great a distance."[*]

We must hone this kind of perceptiveness—this observational, interpretive care and consideration—and expand it beyond clothing to all aspects of the individual. Being good at creating social openings requires you to pay creative attention to your potential copeople's whole style—to their interests, tastes, struggles, aspirations, and to how they are exploring or cultivating these things. But if our attention and perceptiveness is blunted, then we'll be unaware of the awesome details—the details of your coperson's efforts in dress, of her choice of music or decor, of her sense of humor, moods, and desires.

Relatedly, awesomeness requires a kind of sympathetic

---

[*] Baudelaire, "The Painter of Modern Life."

understanding that allows us to not only recognize but vibe with expressive action. We cannot divorce our sense of a whole person from our sympathetic impression of their individuality, of the range of particular traits and values they have expressed and explored in our presence. My sense of you—my sensibility and sensitivity with respect to you—depends in part on the image of your laughter at a joke, your response to a song, your willingness to come along. But this sense of mine depends in turn on the range of particular values and styles I'm able to vibe with, appreciate, or be moved and impressed by. We must be able to understand and appreciate a range of individualities and how they can be expressed, lest we cut ourselves off from one another and our crews become attenuated and atrophied cliques.

And to achieve this, we need active, creative, and insightful imaginations, ones that we work to orient toward coperson creation. We have to imagine and reimagine ways of creating social openings and taking them up to bring individuals together. We have to practice acting on our creative community-building thoughts and impulses in public, with our families, friends, and neighbors, in our professional lives and daily lives, and for ourselves and one another—the vibrancy of our culture, our cities, our neighborhoods, even our own well-being depends on it.

This means that we have to be bold and put ourselves out there, which isn't always easy or simple. We worry about whether we'll succeed and how people will react. Suckiness can really sting, and when we try to be awesome we can really mess up by being insensitive, imperceptive, overly ambitious, or forgetful. Louis C.K. relates a real-world example of this in a bit about his "awesome possum" T-shirt. Returning to the coffee shop one last time:

> So, here's a weird thing that happened to me. I have this T-shirt, and it says "awesome possum" on it. And it's got a picture of a possum. I know it's stupid, but a friend of mine gave it to me. Fuck you, I bought it. I thought it was cool. But I'd never seen anybody with that same shirt before, with the "awesome possum" shirt, and I was in this coffee place in L.A., you know, like, a coffee—not like Starbucks—like an indie coffee place where all the cool people go. . . . But anyway, yeah, so I was in the coffee place, with the young people . . . and I see this guy, he's, like, twenty years old, and he has the "awesome possum" shirt. Just like mine! So, I went, like, "Hey, nice shirt." And he went, "Pfff." And he walked away, like I'm a piece of shit. And I stood there, and I was so mad, I just thought, "Fuck him, man, we have the same shirt!" it's an unusual shirt!*

Having the same unusual shirt is a little social opening that Louis C.K. recognized and initiated. When the guy said, "Pfff," and walked off, he seemed to epitomize wackness by closing the social opening and dismissing the thought that it's

---

* From Louis C.K.'s HBO comedy special *Shameless* (2007), dir. Stephen J. Santos.

kind of awesome that they have the same "awesome possum" shirt. That hurts, but it's also disillusioning. If we can't connect over a silly T-shirt, then how can we connect at all? Louis C.K. understandably retreated, cursing the "cool" coffee shop and its too-cool inhabitants.

But that isn't the whole story. When Louis C.K. looked down to affirm the worth of his "awesome possum" shirt, he realized he wasn't actually wearing it. He forgot. What seemed to be a case of someone else's wackness was actually his own failed attempt to create a social opening.

Sometimes our wires get crossed, the timing isn't right, or we just don't connect and vibe. But we can't let suckiness and failed awesomeness get us down. It's all too easy to lose touch with the value of being awesome and fall into sucky habits, revert to fake-assery, self-efface, or think in or unreflectively adopt stereotypes. It's unnerving how repeatedly we need to be awakened to one another's individuality, shocked out of our blinding and false familiarity with one another and our complacency with ourselves. We must constantly be returned to the sense of worth, wonder, and beauty that even a perfect stranger can evoke in us—and that animates us in our own pursuit of awesomeness.

Awesomeness is the bell that a free people must endlessly sound; it's the caffeine we must crave lest we get headachy, tired, cranky—the small price we must pay to become human again and again. The ethics of awesomeness is an ethics of aspiration and communal imagination: The imagination must be cultivated; the culture must be imagined.

Too many of us live as if this kind of imaginative community building doesn't matter, isn't worthy of appreciation, as if it's something we can just leave to someone else, or simply kick to the side. When you suck, you not only fail to inject your own life-giving energy into the thing, you actually vacuum life out of it because of everyone's more or less subtle awareness that the thing *needs* your presence and contribution to live and breathe. Such suckiness issues from a false sense of culture and community as a static thing, as simply there whenever you need it, as your bottomless source of connection—as if it's not something we create and confirm together in every awesome interaction, as if our bonds need no light or water or chemicals, or as if it's something you can just pay or vote for, or always find waiting for you on Netflix. This kind of existential disposition to suck can do more than cast a pall over a party or add a sour note to an otherwise beautiful connection. It can make others feel that the spirit of awesomeness is not worth tapping into, that being down is not essential, or that you can just let others bring everyone together. It's the black hole of the suckiverse—one that can pull entire crews, cultures, and societies into its vast nothingness.

I hope that together we can move further and further away from this black hole, but it's too soon to know what will happen. The ethics of awesomeness gives us a new and vibrant ideal—a kind of valuing orientation or sensibility, one that we can adopt and live, breathe, and see by. It's a way of life that is still unfolding before our eyes, and we're in the process of making it happen through social, cultural, institutional, and personal change. From our current vantage point, we don't really know what life would look like if we were more awesome more often. What would we care to think, read, and write about? What would we love to do? Whom would we love to be around? What kinds of communities and neighborhoods would we build? What kinds of movements and collectives would we start or support? What kinds of cultures and societies would we create?

I don't have the answers to these questions, and we can only find them together. One thing is for sure: I'm down to find out.

Acknowledgments

Writing this book provided many social openings. Whenever I brought it up—at a party, a dinner, with academic friends—people responded with ideas, examples, insights, and enthusiasm. Thanks to the many friends, colleagues, and copeeps who helped me along. Special thanks to Ross Andersen, Sinan Dogramaci, Daniel Fogal, Ben Jahn, Ed Lake, Stan Parish, Laurie Paul, Jeff Sebo, Erin Thompson, and Clinton Tolley.

Thanks to Amanda Jaquin for helping me design the diagram of awesomeness and suckiness. Her graphic style makes it sing.

Thanks so much to Sara Bershtel, who read a very early draft and introduced me to Mel Flashman. This book would not exist without Mel, who is far more awesome than she thinks.

I'm so lucky that Meg Leder was enthusiastically down to work on this book with me. Her editorial insight and support, along with Shannon Kelly, vastly improved the book. Thanks to the rest of the Penguin Books team for all of their help.

Around the time that I started thinking through these

ideas, Aaron James was visiting NYU, where I was lecturing. I asked him if he'd have lunch with me so I could tell him about my nascent project. He agreed and we talked for a solid two hours. Since then he's been an awesome mentor. Thanks to Aaron for his early encouragement and guidance.